TEEN
LIBRARY
EVENTS

TEEN
LIBRARY
EVENTS

A Month-by-Month Guide

KIRSTEN EDWARDS

Greenwood Professional Guides for Young Adult Librarians
C. Allen Nichols and Mary Anne Nichols, Series Editors

GREENWOOD PRESS
Westport, Connecticut • London

Library of Congress Cataloging-in-Publication Data

Edwards, Kirsten, 1965–
    Teen library events : a month-by-month guide / Kirsten Edwards.
        p. cm.—(Greenwood professional guides for young adult librarians,
    ISSN 1532–5571)
    Includes bibliographical references and index.
    ISBN 0–313–31482–9 (alk. paper)
    1. Young adults' libraries—Activity programs—United States. 2. Public
    libraries—Services to teenagers—United States. I. Title. II. Series.
    Z718.5.E35   2002
    027.62′6—dc21   00–052430

British Library Cataloguing in Publication Data is available.

Library of Congress Catalog Card Number: 00–052430
ISBN: 0–313–31482–9
ISSN: 1532–5571

First published in 2002

Greenwood Press, 88 Post Road West, Westport, CT 06881
An imprint of Greenwood Publishing Group, Inc.
www.greenwood.com

Printed in the United States of America

The paper used in this book complies with the
Permanent Paper Standard issued by the National
Information Standards Organization (Z39.48–1984).

10 9 8 7 6 5 4 3

Copyright Acknowledgments

The author and publisher gratefully acknowledge permission for use of the following
material:

Figure 2.1, "Love Bites booklist," used by permission of Lesley Knieriem.

This book is dedicated to
Robyn L. (because we said we would)
and to
Lorraine Jackson Burdick,
inspiration, friend, and partner in crime.

CONTENTS

SERIES FOREWORD

We firmly believe in young adult library services and advocate for teens whenever we can. We are proud of our association with Greenwood Press and grateful for their acknowledgment of the need for additional resources for teen-serving librarians. We intend for this series to fill those needs, providing useful and practical handbooks for library staff. Readers will find some theory and philosophical musings, but for the most part, this series will focus on real-life library issues with answers and suggestions for front-line librarians.

Our passion for young adult librarian services continues to reach new peaks. As we travel to present workshops on the various facets of working with teens in public libraries, we are encouraged by the desire of librarians everywhere to learn what they can do in their libraries to make teens welcome. This is a positive sign since too often libraries choose to ignore this underserved group of patrons. We hope you find this series to be a useful tool in fostering your own enthusiasm for teens.

Mary Anne Nichols
C. Allen Nichols
Series Editors

ACKNOWLEDGMENTS

Nearly all of these programs were created for the King County Library System in Washington State. This quantity and quality of young adult programming would not be possible without an administration that also believes in the importance of good programs for teens and a Library Board's unwavering support of the same.

I would also like to acknowledge the debt of gratitude I owe to youth services librarians throughout the years for advice and clever ideas and to my good fortune in being able to work with so many of them at the King County Library System and as part of the Washington Library Association.

INTRODUCTION

In the United States and in other parts of the world, we are witnessing a new phenomenon: a teen subculture. Once the teen years were simply part of the transitional time from childhood to adulthood. Now, however, teens—or young adults (YA), as librarians like to call them—are a separate entity. They are almost, as Patricia Hersch titled her seminal book, *A Tribe Apart*. Ms. Hersch provides compelling evidence that teenagers in the United States do present us with a distinct service community. All youth are persons in transition, and all adults who work with them want primarily to help bring them safely to adulthood. Librarians today have more resources than ever to understand, approach, and work with this new tribe. I hope this small book will be a useful tool for the children's services librarian, the young adults' librarian, or the adult services librarian who wishes to initiate YA programming in his or her library.

This book contains a month-by-month description of programs an individual librarian can create for teens. In each case the librarian who wants to should be able to copy a program exactly, but with plenty of flexibility to tailor it to local needs. As much as possible, especially with craft programs, I have provided detailed instructions, lists of materials needed, and the like.

All the programs in this book have been "teen tested" in the sense that they've been used in the small northwestern community libraries where I work. Although it is true that teens have many developmental features in common, I am unwilling to concede that there is a "typical teen" any more than there is a typical 7 or 38 year old. People are diverse—not only in race, gender, or sexual preference but also in interests, goals, habits, and world views. Therefore, rather than give examples of rave reviews from individual teens for certain programs, in this book I show how a particular program meets the developmental needs or desires common to teenagers, or how it can be useful in forging a link between the local librarian and the community of teens she serves. No book, certainly not this handbook, can be a substitute for talking to and being involved with the individual teenagers in the reader's own community.

One popular notion that continued exposure to children—and to the children on the verge of adulthood we call teenagers—will dispell is that of the desire for novelty. Indeed, the common preference of most individuals is for familiarity. The popularity of series titles is a clue. Repetition and variation are useful tools in creating a series of Young Adult programs. This book, designed as a starter kit, includes ways of expanding on the fledgling Young Adult program it will help to create.

Nearly every book carries assumptions about the reader and about how the book will be used. This one is no exception. The first is that the reader wants—in fact, *likes*—to learn. One of the programs mentioned in an upcoming chapter had its inception when a group of teens with whom I was working said that they thought a bookmaking class would be fun. I'm not an expert in bookmaking, but my local library contained helpful books and videos on the topic. When I'd finished reviewing these resources, I taught the young people, providing not only the materials and the opportunity to learn something useful and fun but also the living proof of what a library has to offer. To quote Lois Bujold's mad Miles Vorkosigan, "If I can do it, *you* can do it."

I was concerned that a "getting started" handbook might convey too many assumptions about the reader in terms of expertise, talent, or financial resources. Included in *Teen Library Events* are not only simple starter programs that anyone can do, but more complex ones that require self-training or the hiring or recruiting of an "expert." These appear both set off throughout the text and at the end of certain chapters. Bibliographic aids—both print and electronic—are summarized at the end of the book for the reader's convenience, but they are also mentioned as expert help within the chapters to which they apply. As to the program costs, most can be done inexpensively but very few are free. Where it's possible, I have recommended the creation of a "craft box." The initial outlay for the basic supplies pays off down the road.

This book's biggest assumption is about you, the reader, wanting to serve youth. You've decided you want to plan, promote, and provide regular programming for teens. You know how to create a booklist and how to do readers' advisory and reference service for all your patrons, including teens. You can cope with the professional ethical requirements regarding freedom of information and the conflicts that often arise as people who are sometimes kids and sometimes adults (and sometimes both at the same time) deal with issues of sexuality, independence, and the consequences of adult choices. Perhaps you're a children's librarian or a reference librarian or a library school student who has decided that a Young Adult Services specialty in public libraries is for you. If, on the other hand, you're coming at this job from out in left field—perhaps you're a volunteer who has been asked to administer a new YA program—set this book down and order (either through Inter-Library Loan or from a bookstore) some of the many excellent basic titles on serving young adults in public libraries and read those first.

I hope that this book will be especially useful for the librarian just starting a Young Adult program. The motivation for writing it came from a friend who wanted to start a YA program at her small, independent library but didn't know where to begin. I hope this book will be a help to her and other librarians like her. It may also, however, be useful to the experienced Young Adult Services librarian who can use it as a handy reference tool for ideas when time and staff are limited.

1

JANUARY

Traditionally the New Year begins with new resolutions and a chance for a new beginning. In many school systems, students come back from winter break and end the school term sometime in January or early February. This chapter discusses using the Michael L. Printz Award for Excellence in Young Adult Literature (which is awarded in January at the midwinter ALA conference) to connect with teens and their teachers. Booktalks are briefly discussed as well. Two display ideas—one designed to market the Printz Award and the other to spark teen ideas and opinions—are offered. Optional programs include a simple bookmaking project and getting a book discussion club started. Keep in mind that when it comes to advertising or preparing for any given program, you'll want to give yourself plenty of advance time. Be prepared to read January's instructions in December, and February's in January.

As most of us are aware, there are three essential parts to any program, only one of which is the presentation. The first two are the advertising and the set-up. When you start Young Adult programming from scratch, you'll need to be patient—attendance is often poor at the beginning—and flexible. You'll want to generate interest and involvement on the part of teens. For this reason I include the Book Discussion Club as an optional program. It's moderately time consuming and expensive. If you're starting from scratch, you may want to lay the groundwork with

Figure 1.1
Michael Printz Award letter

[Name of Teacher]
[School Name & Address]

[Date]

Dear Sir [or Ma'am]

   Once again the American Library Association will choose a book that exemplifies literary excellence in young adult literature and give it the Michael L. Printz
Award. [Use the *www.ala.org/yalsa* Printz Award site to briefly describe last year's
winner.]
   I've enclosed a flyer highlighting the award that I hope you'll display in your
classroom. I've sent a copy to the other English teachers, the school librarian,
and the principal. We're very excited about showcasing the best in teen literature
at [Name of your library] and hope you'll encourage your students to visit us and
check out what we have to offer. [If you're offering the Make Your Own Best Book
program in January, mention it here and include flyers.]
   [Conclude by describing what services your local library has to offer teachers
and their teenage students: help with class projects, booklists, booktalks, special
teacher library cards, and library visits.] As the school year progresses, I'll be in
touch with flyers and information about other library programs that may be of
interest to you and your students.

According to the American Library Association's website, "A NEW AWARD
FOR A NEW MILLENNIUM: The Michael L. Printz Award is an award for a
book that exemplifies literary excellence in Young Adult literature. It is
named for a Topeka, Kansas, school librarian who was a long-time active
member of the Young Adult Library Services Association." For more information about the award, visit *http://www.ala.org/yalsa/printz/*.

   Many schoolteachers think Young Adult novels are merely series romances or packaged teen thrillers and movie tie-ins. But librarians know
that Young Adult literature can also exemplify excellent writing and unfor-
gettable stories. The annual Michael Printz Award winner can be a helpful
introduction of good YA literature to high school and upper middle school
English teachers.

   If you're expanding an existing Young Adult program, you could tie in the
award with offers to teachers to booktalk past (and possible) Printz winners.
Or you could use it as the starting point for a book discussion club in which
students "Pick the Printz" and discuss which book really is the best Young
Adult novel.

   You can print out the website information to create a catchy bulletin board
display, adding copies of the Printz Award winner, runners up, and past
winners. See Figure 1.1 for a sample letter that can be used for announcing
this type of program to teachers, the school librarian, and the principal.

more simple programs and work up to this later in the year. I've also discovered that getting the support of the local high school teachers and school librarian gives this kind of program a real jump-start.

PRINTZ AWARD DISPLAY

Begin by creating a Printz Award display (see Figure 1.2 for a sample poster) with titles of books to check out. On the display poster, leave a space for teens to write in the name of their choice for winner and also to write comments. Be sure to keep pens or pencils handy by the display. Figure 1.3 shows a simple pattern you can use to make a holder that staples to a bulletin board to hold pens or flyers.

QUESTION BOARD

As you set up the Printz Award display, you might also want to begin a year-long program called a Question Board. I first heard about the idea from the sterling Young Adult Services librarian Evie Wilson Lingbloom. It's fast, simple, and easy to do and jump-starts teen involvement. Teens, like everyone else, enjoy and participate more in a program for which they have a sense of ownership, and this is a first step toward that goal. Take a large (11" × 14") sheet of paper and write a question on it, for example, "What's your New Year's Resolution? If any?" Break up that big blank space by scrawling *your* resolution or "Heck, no! I'm already perfect!" As you set it up, smile and ask any teens in the building to contribute.

More ideas for questions, plus a whole lot of inspiration for doing a Young Adult program, can be found in Evie Wilson Lingbloom's *Hanging Out at Rocky Creek: A Melodrama in Basic Young Adult Services in Public Libraries* (Scarecrow Press, 1994). You can also find some great ideas for Question Boards in the book *Journal to the Soul for Teenagers* by Rose Offner (Celestial Arts, 1999). If it doesn't offend your librarian's instincts for book preservation, buy a copy to take apart: Many of the pages make excellent and attractive Question Board displays as is.

Be sure to print out a brief explanation of what the Question Board is, including the expectations you have. For example: "Step right up & give us your opinion. No need to sign it! Wise guys are welcome, but this is a public space—no rude language or hate speech is tolerated." If the ground rules are ignored—one example I experienced was gang signs—simply mark out the unruly sign with a heavy black marker.

Figure 1.2
Printz poster

Michael L. Printz Award

The Michael L. Printz Award is an award for a book that exemplifies literary excellence in young adult literature. It is named for a Topeka, Kansas school librarian who was a long-time active member of the Young Adult Library Services Association.

And the Winner Is:

Which book do you think ought to win the Printz Award for best Young Adult (Teen) Novel? Write in your vote here:

This poster was originally designed to be printed on 8½" × 14" (legal) paper and is to scale.

Figure 1.3
Pocket pattern

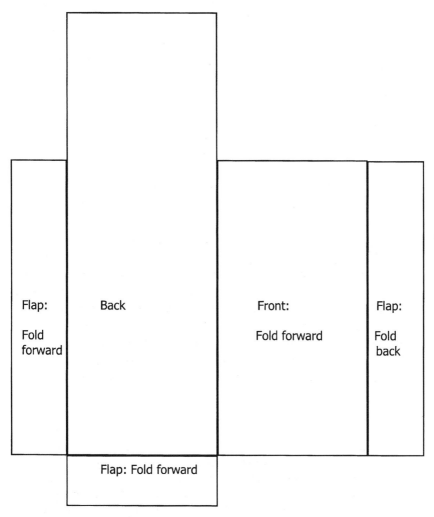

Use any sturdy paper (even old publisher's catalogs) to create simple pockets. Fold and tape together and staple to a bulletin board to hold a couple of pens or pencils or a few flyers.

BOOKTALKS

If you have the time and the ambition, offer to do booktalks for your local high school and upper middle school (grades 7–12) on the Printz Award titles as well as other exceptional Young Adult novels. For resources on just what the titles are, visit the Young Adult Services Divi-

A choice source of great books for teens selected by teens is the New York Public Library's annual publication *Books for the Teen Age*. Order your copy from the Office of the Branch Libraries, The New York Public Library, 455 Fifth Ave., New York, NY 10016. Visit their website at *http://www.nypl.org/branch/teen/Teenlink.html* for sample entries. You can also access Best Books for Young Adults from the YALSA homepage at *http://www.ala.org/yalsa/booklists/*.

sion (YALSA) of the American Library Associations' web page and use the *Best Books for Young Adults* booklists.

If you're already an experienced booktalker, the key point is to use the Printz Award to work with local high school English teachers. As more schools begin to require outside reading material, this is an opportunity to expand many teachers' ideas about Young Adult literature while sharing some of the wealth with their students. If you're a complete novice, however, booktalking is a skill well worth any time you spend acquiring it. The major skill involved is the same one children's librarians use at storytime and other librarians use when making presentations to their Library Board: how to engage an audience. Although performing arts talent may make things easier, it's no requirement: Taking the time to learn the skill and plenty of practice will see anyone through a good booktalk. Local resources to help you acquire this skill include storytelling guilds, toastmaster groups, and colleges that offer storytelling or speech courses.

Dr. Joni Richards Bodart's classic *Booktalk!* volumes 1–5 (vol. 5: Wilson, 1993) give many sample booktalks for novice and experienced booktalkers to use, plus tips and tricks. Ms. Bodart moderates a listserve at *www.egroups.com*. Search for it under "booktalking." It's a helpful group where you can "learn more about booktalking. Improve your writing and presenting skills. Find ideas to jazz up your booktalking presentations. Meet someone (actually, lots of them!) to talk to with about booktalks and booktalking. Join teachers and librarians from all over the country, and exchange booktalks, bibliographies, tips, problems, questions, ideas, and even tall tales of wonderful or awful experiences." Carol Littlejohn's *Talk That Book!* (Linworth, 1999) offers loads of information for getting started, plus a range of titles for audiences ranging from elementary school to adult. For every other question, see Chapter 6, "Don't Tell, Sell" in Patrick Jones's indispensable *Connecting Young Adults and Libraries*, 2nd ed. (Neal Schuman, 1998). You can also visit his website at *http://www.connectingya.com/*.

BOOKMAKING

The small bookmaking program described here has been used with several groups of teens at different libraries and has been successful in all its variants. We've made "Romantic Heart Books" for Valentine's Day gifts, "Antique Autograph Books" as part of an American history program, and "Personal Journals" to tie in with a middle school's journal-writing assignment. Although craft programs are the staples of children's summer camps and activities nationwide, it's necessary to look to adult arts and crafts to find programs with teen appeal. It's not that you don't want the project to be a fun, achievable, hands-on activity (of course you do); the idea is to teach a real skill or to make something intrinsically interesting or useful. The bookmaking instructions provided in Figure 1.4 are based on actual bookbinding techniques used in ancient Japan. Once the basic techniques have been mastered, the student can move on to more complicated projects and eventually create "real" books if he or she so desires.

To advertise a Make Your Own Best Book program, you'll want to send letters to local English teachers, art teachers, and homeschool associations. Write to your local newspapers and ask for your program to be included in their Community Events column. However, one of the best tools is a visual display of the finished product. Make sample copies of the books and display them next to the sign advertising the program. I'll discuss linking programming to tabletop displays and marketing books in greater detail in Chapter 2 (February) but here's an option if you have a display cabinet: Use the sample copies, plus some of the materials that you used to make them, to create an eye-catching display. Add a sign that says, "Want to make one? It's free! Ask at the checkout (or reference) desk."

TEEN BOOK DISCUSSION GROUP

You can also use the booktalks and the Printz Award to kick off a new teen book discussion club at your library. If, however, you don't have a group of teens clamoring for just that experience, plus plenty of groundwork laid, you'll find that this project will start very slowly and may not begin to pay off until six months or a year down the road. Assuming that you're willing to give it a try, here's a simple program outline.

"Pick the Printz—with Pizza," a kick-off program for a book discussion group, should begin with you contacting local high school and mid-

Figure 1.4
How to make a book

Materials (per book)

- 2 cardboard or mat board covers (any size)
- 2 cover papers (+1" larger than the board covers on every side)
- 10 to 25 inside papers or "pages" (less ¼" than the board covers on all sides EXCEPT one: the spine or hinge side)
- 2 endpapers (less ½" than the board covers on every side)
- glue (either YES! or some other paste or simple glue sticks; about 1 per book)
- hole punch or an awl, hammer and a wooden board
- scrap paper (old magazines work well)
- weights (book sale books work well)
- 18" of cord and a large tapestry needle
- two 6" lengths of ribbon
- scissors, rulers, tape and a pencil

1. Make a hinge

A. Measure 1" in from the edge of the board. This will become the top cover, the other will be the back.
B. Cut 1" off. This will be the hinge. Set aside.
C. Measure another $\frac{1}{8}$" off the larger piece, cut off, and discard. This provides a narrow gap for the hinge.

2. Glue front and back cover board to cover paper

A. Measure 1" in on all sides of the two pieces of cover paper with your pencil. These will be guidelines for laying down the cover boards.
B. Glue the back of the large piece of the front cover board and line it up with your guideline when you place it on the cover paper.
C. Glue the hinge board and line it up with the guide lines as you place it on the paper. There should be a gap between the two pieces.
D. Glue the back cover board to the second piece of cover paper in the same way.

3. Finish wrapping the cover

A. Always fold first to make a crease, then glue down

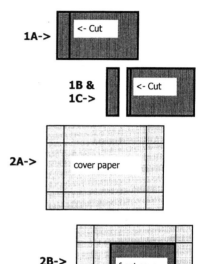

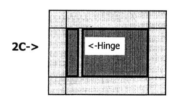

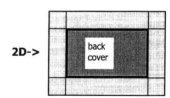

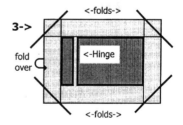

4. Add ribbons

Tape a ribbon on the inside of each cover so that part sticks out the far side.

5. Add endpapers

A. Take the endpapers, glue them, and place them down over the ribbon and folded edges on the inside of each book cover.

B. Turn the top cover over and feel for the slight indentation where there is a gap between the hinge and the main cover. Run your fingernail gently along it to crease and mark the hinge.

C. Optional: If you have the time, slip both book covers between sheets of scrap paper and weight down under a heavy weight for 4 hours.

6. Put holes in the cover and interior pages

A. Take the front cover and measure in ½" from the hinge side and 2" from the top and bottom. Mark these intersections. They will be the holes through which you thread cord and fasten the book together.

B. Using hole punch, punch holes where you've marked.

C. Place the bottom cover under the top and use it as a guide to punch matching holes through the back cover.

D. Again using the top cover as a guideline, line up the interior pages together against the spine (hinge side) of the front cover. Mark the spot for the holes and hole punch about 3 to 4 pages at a time, checking that they line up with the front cover as you go along

E. Optional: Measure, mark, and line up all the pieces, and punch each hole through the entire set with one hard blow of the hammer on the awl.

7. Putting it all together / Sewing the book up

A. Place the pieces together: top cover, pages, and bottom cover with the two holes lined up.

B. Take the cord, thread it onto the needle, and run the cord through the top hole from the front side. Leave about 3" sticking out, but pull taut. The needle and cord are now on the back side.

C. Bring the needle up through the bottom hole from the back side. Pull taut. The cord is now on the front side.

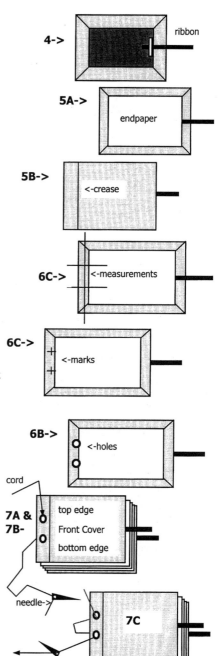

4-> ribbon

5A-> endpaper

5B-> <-crease

6C-> <-measurements

6C-> <-marks

6B-> <-holes

cord

7A & 7B- top edge / Front Cover / bottom edge

needle->

7C

9

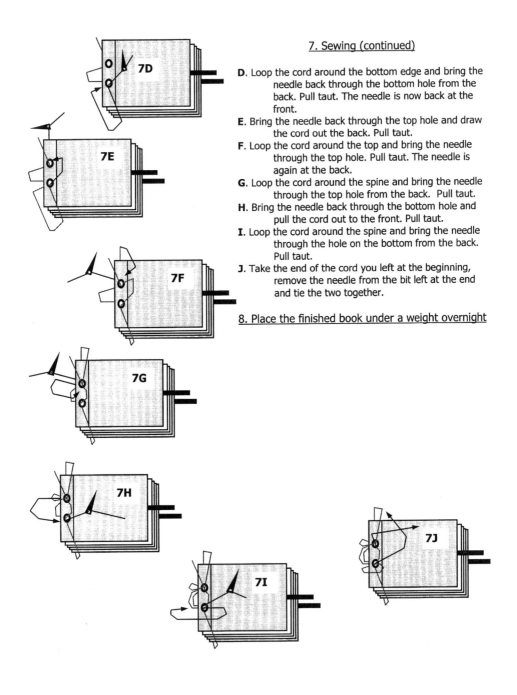

7. Sewing (continued)

D. Loop the cord around the bottom edge and bring the needle back through the bottom hole from the back. Pull taut. The needle is now back at the front.

E. Bring the needle back through the top hole and draw the cord out the back. Pull taut.

F. Loop the cord around the top and bring the needle through the top hole. Pull taut. The needle is again at the back.

G. Loop the cord around the spine and bring the needle through the top hole from the back. Pull taut.

H. Bring the needle back through the bottom hole and pull the cord out to the front. Pull taut.

I. Loop the cord around the spine and bring the needle through the hole on the bottom from the back. Pull taut.

J. Take the end of the cord you left at the beginning, remove the needle from the bit left at the end and tie the two together.

8. Place the finished book under a weight overnight

Figure 1.5
Book discussion letter

[If you've decided to kick off the New Year with a book discussion group, insert the following paragraph.]

In addition, we'd like to encourage teens who enjoy reading great books to join our new Teen Book Discussion Club. At our first meeting—"Pick the Printz—with Pizza!"—we'll be discussing our all-time favorite Young Adult novels while munching on pizza and soda. [Include the date, time, and location as well as a flyer.] I hope you share this opportunity with your students.

dle school English teachers. If you haven't already gotten a list of all these teachers' names, now's the time to do so. Include a paragraph (see Figure 1.5) in your letter about the Printz Award contest (Fig. 1.2) letting them know about the book discussion group opportunity for their students. Include a sample flyer (see Figure 1.6). Write a letter to local homeschooling groups, including your flyer and inviting their teenage children to attend. Place these flyers in the library. I've also made bookmark-size versions of the flyer (see Figure 1.7) and asked library staff to place one in any book, magazine, CD, or video checked out by a teen in the two weeks prior to the actual kick-off date. You'll also want to send a letter to local papers for their Community Events column. When and if you go in to the schools to booktalk the Printz Award books, be sure to mention the upcoming book discussion club, indicate that munchies will be provided, and hand out bookmarks or flyers to interested teens.

If you want to be truly ambitious and can spare the time away from your library, see if the school librarian and principal are willing to let you offer this book discussion program after school in the school library as a regular, monthly after-school event. You can even continue the program during the summer or over long vacation breaks at your own library.

On the day the book discussion group meets, you should gather munchies, pens and paper, and plenty of great books that you can discuss. I've included some titles in some of this chapter's offset material, but your best bet is titles that have some kind of impact, controversy, or twist that can spark discussion and, if you're all going to read the same book, are easy to access. As teens arrive, provide munchies and chat. Many will probably know one another, but it's a good idea to open the meeting with introductions and some form of icebreaker game (see Figure 1.8 for a sample Bingo board). Ask the teens questions about what brought them to the meeting and how they heard of it. (Take notes—

Figure 1.6
Book Discussion Club flyer

(Your Library) Teen Book Discussion Club

Do you love books? Would you like to get together with other teens who enjoy reading? To discuss interesting & unusual books in a relaxed atmosphere with drinks & munchies? If the answer is "Yes!", join us every other week at (your location) for the (Your Library) Teen Book Discussion Group.

January - May Schedule:

Tues., January X
Topic: Pick the Printz—With Pizza! What is the best Young Adult (Teen) novel of all time?

Tues., February X
Topic: To Be Announced

Tues. March X
Topic: To Be Announced

Tues., April X
Topic: To Be Announced

Tues. May X
Topic: To Be Announced

Tues. June X
Topic: To Be Announced

Every Fourth Tuesday
(or whatever works for your library)
at the
(Your Library)
(Name & title of your contact person * Library address * phone number)
Reasonable accommodation for individuals with disabilities will be provided. Please contact the library prior to the event if you require accommodation.

This flyer was originally designed to be printed on 8½" × 14" (legal) paper and is to scale.

Figure 1.7
Book Discussion Club bookmark

 (Your Library) Teen Book Discussion Club

Do you love books? Would you like to get together with other teens who enjoy reading? Would you enjoy discussing interesting and unusual books in a relaxed atmosphere with drinks and munchies? If the answer is "Yes!", join us every other week for the (Your Library) Teen Book Discussion Group.

Tuesday, January X
(Your Time)
(Your library's location)

Our first club meeting: Pick the Printz—With Pizza! Enjoy pizza & good company as we second guess the award - which book *really* is the best YA novel?

Each Month:

Every 4th Tues. (or your date) at the (Your Library) January X, February X, March X, April X, May X, & June X

(Your contact person's name & title * Your library's address * phone number)

Reasonable accommodation for individuals with disabilities will be provided. Please contact the library prior to the event if you require accommodation.

Four such bookmarks will fit on one 8½" × 14" (legal) sized paper.

Figure 1.8
"Getting to Know You" Bingo

Bingo!

Fill in the names of anyone in the group to whom these statements apply (names can be used more than once). When you have a row across, down, or diagonally: "Bingo!"

Flosses every day	Has met someone famous	Has been to an amuse-ment park	Likes to read	Likes broccoli (at least a little)
Thinks Leonardo DiCaprio is annoying	Thinks Leonardo DiCaprio is cute	Likes the color blue	Hates liver	Saw any movie more than three times
Hates to read	Likes romance	Likes fantasy or SF	Has traveled out-side the U.S.	Can remember his or her dreams
Likes mysteries	Plans on traveling next summer	Has a dog (Which kind?)	Has a cat (Which kind?)	Has a brother or sister (How many?)
Would look different if they could	Wears T-shirts	Is an only child	Knows what he or she wants to be as an adult	Has long hair

One place that has provided a variety of suggestions for book discussion titles and ideas is the Children's and Young Adult's e-mail listserv "Pubyac." You can visit its homepage at *http://www.pallasinc.com/pubyac*. Sign-up instructions for the listserv can be found in the bibliography at the end of this book. Among the titles recommended by the librarians on Pubyac are *The Music of Dolphins* by Karen Hesse (Apple, 1998) for younger teens (grades 6–8) and *Rats Saw God* by Rob Thomas (Aladdin Paperbacks, 1996) for older teens (grades 9 and up). The former was a huge hit, sparking a great discussion as one of my groups evenly split among boys and girls as to whether they loved or hated it. But don't expect teens to stick to the beaten track; one new high school book discussion group chose *Dreams of Trespass: Tales of a Harem Girlhood* by Fatima Mernissi (Addison-Wesley Longman, 1995)—a complex adult nonfiction title.

you'll find out what, if any, of your advertising works.) Find out what their expectations are. Ask each teen to describe his or her favorite book and why. Follow up by trying to reach a consensus about what makes a good book. Act as a moderator to keep the ball rolling and to smooth out rough edges, but let the teens "take over" the meeting.

During the last 15 to 20 minutes of the meeting, ask the teens what they'd prefer for the next meeting: everyone reading the same book, or everyone reading the same type of book and talking about the genre. The latter is your best choice if neither the library collection nor the teens can afford to provide the same books for everyone. Sometimes a local bookstore can be induced to sponsor a teen book discussion club and provide free books, but it's best not to count on it. Once next month's agenda is set, find out which teen or pair of teens would like to lead the discussion. Provide a framework for the participants of the types of questions a leader might ask or background material they'd want to check out. In the former case, ask questions such as, "If what happened to the protagonist happened to you, how would you react? Do you think the author got it right?" In the latter case, offer library reference materials about a particular genre or magazine articles about a particular author. With a shy or younger group, this easing of the leadership roles into the hands of the teens could wait until next month's meeting.

COMMUNITY RESOURCES

Ready for February? Not yet. Now is the time, if you're planning a summer reading program in addition to a once-a-month offering of programs for teens, to begin gathering material for prizes and getting out among the community. Free magazines and books that have teen appeal (including donations to a "Friends" book sale) can be set aside in a box marked "Prizes." If your Friends of the Library group can afford it, ask them for a commitment to sponsor part of your summer program. Read ahead in this book and ask yourself which programs you might want to use this year; then determine what kind of funding the Friends group could help with. Write up a letter asking for, say, $40 for the tie-dye program kit, $20 for supplies for the Ice-Cream Social (both are described in Chapter 7), and another $30 for three $10 gift certificates to local businesses that you can give away as prizes during the summer. You'll want to briefly explain the importance of programs for teens at your library and how the Friends' financial contribution will make the programs possible.

Your community's local businesses are another potential source of assistance. If you begin with either the bookmaking craft or the book discussion club, go around to local businesses with flyers asking if you can display them in their places of business. It makes a good reason to make that first contact, as often a manager's permission is required. Even if you don't have the excuse, make the time to introduce yourself and your mission (connecting teens with books, with reading, and with their library) and ask if it would it be acceptable to contact the business in the spring about donating a prize or prizes for the teen summer reading program. Swap business cards or trade name, title, and contact information and save this in your notebook or computer file. In May you'll be calling, writing, or visiting the business again, asking for specific prizes: a gift certificate, merchandise such as CDs from a music store, a voucher for one free movie rental from a video store, or a free graphic novel or set of comic books from a comic or gaming store.

This will be the first step in what may prove to be a long-lasting relationship with your community businessmen and businesswomen. To some extent, getting the prizes is just the icing on the cake. Because either at this visit or the next, you'll want to ask if, in addition to supporting the community's library and teens, the business owner or manager would be willing to share his or her expertise at a library program or seminar for teens sometime down the road, perhaps in the summer. A gift certificate or a CD is pretty easy to give; a person's time, when he or she is already loaded down with commitments to work, family, and the community, can be a tall order.

I must admit, this is far and away the most difficult job for me, but for every four or five (or sometimes nine or ten) "No thanks" I hear, I get one adult who is willing to share his or her skills and experience with young people. Now *that's* a great resource.

2

FEBRUARY

In this chapter we'll focus on continuing the groundwork begun in January and lay the foundations for a teen volunteer group. The program is a simple guessing game that can be used to identify local teens interested in library events.

From last month you'll want to continue your Question Board, updating it with something new. Depending on how fast it fills up and how much time you have, you could change it weekly. Either way, mix in questions that not only provoke comment (such as, "If you won a million dollars, what would you do?") but also tie in with your programming and your displays and help you connect with your teen clientele. For example, "What's the music you love?" can help you update your music collection. Save the Question Board and when the new titles you've ordered arrive, create a new item display: "You asked for it, you got it!"

Unfortunately, most libraries don't have the budget to advertise their programs on prime-time teen television. Nor can we pay for plugs on the local rock, rap, or country station. The latter can sometimes be surprisingly approachable (don't bank on it, though), but if you're starting a program series, a book discussion club, or a summer reading program, send these radio stations a letter asking for a public service announce-

Figure 2.1
Love Bites booklist

LOVE BITES!
Stories to break your heart.

Tenderness by Robert Cormier. A runaway girl looking for love finds tenderness in a strange place - the heart of a serial killer who's already murdered several girls like her...

Children of the River by Linda Crew. Sundara had fled her war-torn Cambodian homeland four years ago when she was just 13, leaving behind her family and the boy she had always loved. Now she is safe in the U.S., struggling to fit in at high school and still remain loyal to her culture and traditions. Then she meets Jon, who seems different from other American boys. Can she be with him and not betray her past and her people?

Running Loose by Chris Crutcher. Louie has everything he could want: He's a senior in high school with a car, a starting spot on the football team, good friends & the girl of his dreams. But his hopes & dreams are shattered as everything he knows about sportsmanship, fair play, love & life are snatched away from him.

The Silver Kiss by Annette Curtis Klause. Simon is the only one who seems to understand Zoe's brooding thoughts on her dying mother. He too is obsessed with death, since he is cursed with immortality as one of the Undead — a vampire. For hundreds of years he has been seeking revenge on his brother for the gruesome murder of their mother. Dare Simon ask Zoe to finally set him free from his eternal chase and unbearable loneliness?

Blood & Chocolate by Annette Curtis Klause. Love is hard enough when you're in high school, but when you're a werewolf and the sensitive guy you adore is "meat" - a human boy - life can get really tricky. Can a predator ever really love her prey?

The Darkangel by Meredith Pierce. Never had Aeriel seen anything as evil as the Darkangel, the Vampyre who has already imprisoned the souls of 13 innocent brides in a chain around his neck. But never has Aeriel seen anything so beautiful or magnificent either, with a spark of goodness buried beneath his cruelty. Aeriel is only a servant, but she holds the key to the Darkangel's damnation - or his salvation.

The Things I Did Last Summer by Erika Tamar. Summer romances are always temporary, but Andy thinks that things are going to be different for him and Susan. She is three years older than him, for one thing; and for another, he suspects that she's in trouble. Will his newfound journalistic skills and his love for Susan be enough to rescue her? Or is it Andy who needs rescuing?

Appointment with a Stranger by Jean Thesman. Handsome, tender Tom Hurley saves Keller from drowning & turns her life upside down. Drew jealously tries to point out how strange and shadowed her new love is, but Keller refuses to see the truth...

Rats Saw God by Rob Thomas. Sophomore year was perfect for Steve. He's living with his dad, the famous astronaut. He has found a crowd of friends who are cool, funny & smart. Best of all, he's in love with the greatest girl in the world. But by his senior year, Steve is depressed and on the verge of flunking out. His only hope to graduate is to tell the story of how he got this way...

The Road Home by Ellen Emerson White. Rebecca, a young surgical nurse, has survived Vietnam. She knows she's luckier than most of the young men she's seen - killed or mutilated - certainly luckier than Michael - a young soldier she loves who lost both his legs. But both she and Michael are desperately heart-wounded. They may be back in the U.S.A., but they're a long way from home...

Two bookmarks will fit onto one 8½" × 11" (letter) paper.

Use tabletop displays to market your YA collection. For Valentine's Day, why not create a display featuring doomed love? "Love Bites" is a list of heartbreaker romance titles compiled by Lesley Knieriem (YA librarian extraordinaire) and posted to the Yalsa-bk, an on-line group dedicated to discussing YA books and issues. You can find out about this and YALSA's other listservs at *http://www.ala.org/yalsa/professional/yalsalists.html*. See the bibliography at the end of this book for sign-up instructions.

Check out the sample booklist "bookmark" in Figure 2.1. Update the list, deleting titles you don't have and adding some you do, and then print it out on colored paper. Gather the titles together and tuck a bookmark into each one. Place the books in a pretty basket and set the basket on a table or counter where you'll see it often enough to refill as needed.

ment. Most of us need to rely on local newspapers, flyers, and word of mouth. The good news is that word of mouth usually works.

CANDY RAFFLE AND RECRUITMENT DRIVE

The way to get teen word of mouth going for your programs is the same way to increase participation and establish a feeling of ownership—through teen involvement. Hence the February program, which I repeat once each year, is the annual "Guess the number, win the candy" combination program, display, and recruiting drive.

You'll need a tall, clear glass container, inexpensive small candles, some pencils, some ballots, and a ballot box. The latter can be built out of cardboard, duct tape, and wrapping paper or purchased inexpensively at an office supply store. Fill the container with the candies; tape it shut and set it in a location with plenty of teen foot traffic right next to the ballot box.

To create ballots (see Figure 2.2), you'll want slips of paper where teens can write in their names, contact information (phone, e-mail, or snail-mail), and age. Ask them to guess the number of candies in the jar (closest guess wins all the candy; in case of a tie, a random drawing breaks it) and write down at least one thing they loved from the library in the past year: a book, CD, video, or magazine. Save space for one last question: "Would you like to be contacted about future library programs for teens?"

Save the "Yes, I would" responses and create a list (updated yearly) of teens on your mailing list. You'll be able to contact these teens not just for craft programs such as Make Your Own Best Book in January but for work parties (help build the library entry in the local parade for

Figure 2.2
Ballot entry form

💙 Enter to Win! 💙

Every item you loved gets you one guess! Tell us one thing from the library you loved this past year & guess the number of candies. Closest guess wins!

(In the event of a tie, the library staff will draw a winner randomly)

My guess: _____ candies. Last thing I read that I enjoyed (Book, magazine, CD, video, website or comic book): _____

Name: _____ Age: _____

Contact me by ☐ Phone ☐ Letter ☐ E-mail (Check at least one.)

This is my phone number, street address or e-mail address:

_____

_____

Do you want to be contacted about special library programs for teens?

☐ Letter ☐ E-mail (Check at least one)

Two ballots will fit on an 8½" × 11" (letter) paper.

Not all displays need to tie in directly to your programs. If you need (or want) to create additional displays to market your collection, or simply to add visual interest to a bare spot in the library, don't forget that old standby, *Chase's Calendar of Events 2001: The Day-by-Day Directory to Special Days, Weeks and Months* (Contemporary Books, 2000). In addition to being Black History Month (for which *http://www.netnoir.com* can be a useful resource), did you know that February is also National Self-Esteem Month? Some of the more unusual events can provide inspiration for amusing and eye-catching displays!

the kiddies!) and focus groups ("Cool Comics and More of 'Em" sponsored by the local comic book or gaming shop and designed to help build a new comics and/or graphic novel collection). You'll also be able to contact them as helpers for teen programs (the Coffeehouse in April or the Mystery Night in November). Keep communication informal by calling, writing, or e-mailing these young people once a month; alternatively, if they're game and you have the time, organize a monthly meeting of your new teen advisory group.

The only difficulty I had with the candy raffle program is limiting it to teens only. Younger children often wanted to participate—sometimes so badly that the children's librarian had to run a similar contest at the same time. Luckily, this is one game that everyone wins: Teens have their opinion solicited about what (if anything) they love about their library's collection, and they spend nothing but time and attention and win a greater involvement with a community resource.

Don't forget to contact teachers and homeschool associations/parents with a brief letter telling them what your library is offering for teens this month. That regular contact, including reminders of special services you're ready and willing to offer, pays off in the long run.

Don't forget that the much of the public relations (PR) for any given month's program needs to be sent out three to six weeks in advance. The promotional work for March, which is fairly extensive, will need to be done in February.

3

❖❖❖ ❖❖❖ ❖❖❖

MARCH

Although the focus in this month's programming is on making connections with local businesspeople, the topics of marketing, display, and continuity are also covered. March is Youth Art Month as well as American Red Cross Month, and I have a few suggestions for librarians who'd like to connect with these national events to create teen programs.

Continuing activities include updating the Question Board, removing last month's answers and posting a new question that ties in with this month's program: "What would be your dream job or dream career?" Keep gathering prizes—you'll want them come July. Those connections you made with local businesses will begin to pay off, because you'll need to go out into your community for expert help when you put on your first annual Getting a Summer Job program for teens.

GETTING A SUMMER JOB PROGRAM

To start with, contact your local high school's career center. You may be surprised to discover that it has very little to offer teens in the way of summer job assistance. Generally, its focus is on academic pathways to career and college choices. However, the career center can be helpful in publicizing your program to students. Other publicity includes flyers and letters sent directly to the schools, advertisements in local papers, and in-house flyers. One additional place to locate flyers is local businesses—the same ones at which local teens will be trying to get summer jobs and which you will be asking to help with your March program. And don't forget: All those teens who responded "Yes" to your February candy contest and recruiting drive will appreciate a phone call or post-card telling them about this program. See the flyer advertising the program in Figure 3.1.

For many teens, the month of March seems a million years away from June and the end of school. Nonetheless, many employers who hire for the summer begin to make their decisions as early as April or May. For this reason, it helps the teens if they have job-hunting skills early on. Thus, the Getting a Summer Job program covers the following topics:

- Community resources
- Applications and references
- Interviews
- What do employers look for?
- You and the IRS

Turn to your business community to supply the expertise for this information.

Find a local businessman or businesswoman to assist you in this program. As a first step, setting the time and date of the program appropriately is particularly important. Visit your local business community with a selection of dates that work for you—a weekend morning or early afternoon, a weekday and a weekend night—and use their schedule to organize the program.

You'll need at least one local employer (be it the McDonald's, the local farm, the grocery store—whoever regularly employs teens in the summer in your community) to speak to the topic "What do employers look for?" This person will be invaluable in (1) taking and answering questions from teens who attend your program, and (2) providing an interface between teens who are looking (possibly for the first time) for a job and at the world of employers. Ask this businessperson to give a 10-minute talk on what she likes to see in a prospective teen employee. What gets a young person hired? What gets him re-hired or gets him a great reference? Explain to the businessperson that you want the young people in her community to benefit from his or her experience and that

Figure 3.1
Summer Job flyer

GETTING A SUMMER JOB

Want to work this summer?
Want the winning edge in your job hunt?
Find out about:

- Free resources
- Job applications
- Interviews that get you hired
- What employers really look for
- And more!

(Your date and time)
Featuring guest speaker (Name of your local employer)
Free at (Name of Your Library)
(Your Library's address, phone number, etc.)

Reasonable accommodation for individuals with disabilities may be provided.
Please contact the library prior to the event if you require accommodation.

Most of us can't leave the reference desk or local branch to go door-to-door to local businesses. Certainly we can't do so on a regular basis. Yet I've discovered that simply sending letters isn't effective when you need a favor. What works is cold-calling to set up an appointment. Call to find out the manager's or owner's name if you don't already know it. Then call to speak to the owner or manager, identifying yourself concisely but with enough information that he or she knows what you do. Don't ask for your favor or go into detail about your project: Ask for a meeting. Be ready with a date and time—"Say, Friday at 4 P.M." including alternatives such as "That doesn't work? How about next Monday at 11 A.M."—that work well with your schedule. At the meeting make your presentation, asking for assistance. Most local businesspeople are community-minded, and you have the added bonus of being associated with the public library—a generally recognized "good thing." You know that working with teens is rewarding and important. You know that your program, Getting a Summer Job, will pay off for teens, their parents, *and* their employers! So you can and should present with confidence. For more practical information on making those phone calls successfully, try reading *Cold Calling Techniques (That Really Work)* by Stephen Schiffman (Adams Media Corp., 1999).

they'll be much better potential job applicants as a result. Go over the program schedule and be sure to let him or her know that the program will run for about 45 minutes and that she'll be wanted for questions and "expert opinions" both before and after her special segment on the program.

Regarding the topic "Applications and references," you'll want another employer, preferably the largest employer of teens in your community, to provide you with a sample job application. Make enough photocopies to hand out at least two copies to each teen attending the program. If this employer can come and speak about the importance of job applications and references, so much the better. If not, you should spend about 10 minutes going over the main points of the form. Encourage questions. Then turn to your guest speaker, the businesswoman

Looking for teen talent for a one-time production? Call the high school drama teacher to set up a meeting. Explain that you have (or will have) opportunities for her students to volunteer in the community and hone their acting skills. Ask if she'll act as a liaison, recommending students for parts in programs such as Getting a Summer Job or in the Murder in the Library program in the fall. You'll want to prepare a sample letter that she can give students to take home to their parents, explaining who you are, your credentials, and the parameters of this volunteer opportunity (see Figure 3.2).

Figure 3.2
Letter to parents for teen participation

[Date]

Dear Parent:

  [Name of drama teacher] has recommended your teen for participation in a [Name of your library] program, Getting a Summer Job [or, alternatively, Murder in the Library, a live-action mystery game]. This is an opportunity to hone acting skills and to be of service to the community. Your teen will be acting in short skits at [Name of your library] that demonstrate how young job seekers should behave in interviews [or, alternatively, that will make possible the library's special Mystery Night for teens.] I hope your teen will be able to volunteer for [Name of your library]'s program on [date and time].
  If you have any questions or concerns, please don't hesitate to contact me at [Name of your library] at [Your library's address, phone number, and, if applicable, your e-mail address]. I'm generally available at [your shift dates and times].

I mentioned in the previous paragraph. (There's a reason she goes second-to-last in the program.) Ask her to confirm your admonitions about how employers view such application *faux pas* as messy, scrawled, and food-stained forms or using one's mother as a reference.

  For "Interviews" I've tried two techniques that worked. In the first (and by far the most fun), I asked two teens to help me out by doing a "good teen" and "bad teen" skit for the Getting a Summer Job program. I had an active teen volunteer group at the time, but I've also been able to tap the local drama students for talent as well. I have a basic script in which the librarian (as Ms. or Mr. Boss) interviews two prospective teens: Ms. (or Mr.) Great Hire, and Ms. (or Mr.) Not Likely. See the Appendix at the end of this chapter for the sample script. Usually we involve the audience by asking them to point out what each of the teen actors did right (and wrong). This is by far the most entertaining part of the program, and it makes a good introduction to your guest speaker. The group is charged up and happy and ready to be a good audience.

  In the second technique, I used a variation on the humorous script to role-play interviews with volunteers from the audience. As with the skit, this acts as a "tired-of-sitting-and-listening" buster. It's less entertaining than the skit but does get the teens out of their seats and involved. See the Appendix at the end of this chapter for the complete description.

  Naturally, every topic except "Community resources" and "You and the IRS" can be handled by a local businessman or businesswoman. I've discovered, however, that many of the top teen summer employers are

You don't need to be a tax expert to present information on what students need to know about summer jobs and taxes: The IRS has done that for you. Visit its website at *http://www.irs.gov/forms_pubs/pubs/index.htm* and locate the "Student's Guide to Federal Income Tax." If you call the IRS six to eight weeks in advance, they will send you multiple copies of this form. Of course, you'll want to include the local IRS office's phone number in your list of community resources.

in retail—and retail managers are very busy, very over-scheduled folks. If I can get one business leader to participate, I count it a success. And if I repeat the program every two years, I don't strain the resources of any one person but can provide a fresh face at each program.

Addressing "Community resources," however, is the librarian's job. And topping this list of resources is your workplace: the public library. From Internet-based yellow pages to books like *The Totally Awesome Business Book for Kids: With 20 Super Businesses You Can Start Right Now* by Adriane Berg and Arthur Berg Bochner (Newmarket Press, 1995), to your own searching of the government pages of the local phonebook for job-help lines as well as state job corps opportunities for youth, you should be able to compile quite a list of ideas for teens to get started on locating a summer job. Save the file to disk, and update your list as often as you offer this program.

The March program is a particularly good example of the idea of repetition and variation, as is next month's. The teen population isn't a static minority clientele: In seven years or fewer, if no tragedy occurs, every one of your clients will cease to be a teen. For this reason repeating programs annually, or bi- or tri-annually, simply recognizes that new groups of children will be moving into the teen demographic and facing similar issues. Repeating programs like Getting a Summer Job every two or three years ensures that you can not only reach teens who may have missed the program last year but also guarantees that you'll connect with new teenagers. Moreover, programs such as these benefit from repetition and variation: Every other year different local employers can be spotlighted, cycling through the major employers of teens in your community over four, six, or eight years. Each program brings greater awareness of the event among local teens, their parents, and the business community.

Don't forget that each month's programs require at least a four-week head start. You'll be doing PR in March for April's poetry contest and coffeehouse.

Youth Art and the American Red Cross are both celebrated this month. Sponsored by the Council for Art Education (CFAE), Youth Art Month aims to "emphasize the value of art education for all children and to encourage support for quality school art programs." The Art & Creative Materials Institute (ACMI), an international association of art and craft manufacturers, founded CFAE in the early 1980s. According to its website, CFAE runs Youth Art Month at the national level and supports state and local programs. Each year a national student flag design program is held, and the completed flags are flown in Washington, D.C., during March. Librarians, working with their local art educators, can receive assistance from CFAE for their local programs. Events might include hosting an art or craft demonstration by a local professional or turning part of the library or library meeting room into a gallery for local teen artwork. Visit the Youth Art Month website at *http:// www.acminet.org/youth_art_month.htm* to order a free booklet of programming ideas.

Visit the American Red Cross website at *http://www.redcross.org* to see the range of programs offered for youth such as "Babysitter's Training," "First Aid/CPR," and "HIV/AIDS Awareness and Prevention." In addition, there are community programs such as "Til Help Arrives," a 30-minute to 2-hour program about coping with accidents and disasters that would be appropriate for teens. These can be easily found on the Red Cross's Youth Education page at *http://www.redcross.org/youth/edu/index.html*. Your local Red Cross affiliate can give you the names of individuals in your community who are trained to teach such classes and even help set them up. Most classes, however, are not free to the public, which may be a concern in some settings.

APPENDIX: TEEN ACTORS' INTERVIEW SKIT

Script

Characters

Ms. (or Mr.) Great Hire: Dressed neatly in slacks or a skirt or *very* neat jeans, shirt or blouse, shoes and socks, discreet jewelry and makeup (tattoos and piercings covered up), and hair neatly pulled back or otherwise off the face. She or he carries a day-planner or notebook of some kind.

Ms. (or Mr.) Not Likely: Dressed sloppily in torn jeans or scruffy shorts and a T-shirt with some sort of slogan on it. Shoes are flip-flops or scruffy sneakers without socks. If appropriate with your teens, the height of some fashion—such as Hip Hop—taken to extremes would also work well. Hair is loose and messy, makeup is extreme (tattoos or piercings very visible), and jewelry is loud and large. She or he chews gum loudly or has a large sucker of some kind hanging from the mouth.

Ms. (or Mr.) Boss: Wears business suit.

Set

Use three chairs grouped together to the left as the "waiting room." If you have an over-abundance of willing teen actors, by all means add a second desk with a telephone and a teen actor to be the secretary who announces the applicants. Just right of center, place a desk with a chair behind it (for Ms. Boss) and another in front of it. Add desk accoutrements (telephone, papers, etc.) as you like, but be sure to have two sheets of paper for the two candidates' job applications.

Skit

The skit begins as Ms. Boss arrives, takes center stage, and announces that she's hiring summer interns for her company, "McInfo," and she has two appointments today. She asks the audience to be her hiring committee and help her decide between the two. [Note: The actors will "freeze" at various points as she asks the audience to critique different parts of the scenario.] She takes her seat behind the desk, and the two teen actors take their seats in the waiting area.

Ms. Boss: [Stands up and addresses the audience] I have two candidates for this job. I need someone to do data entry over the summer and maybe pick up a few other office tasks if he or she proves reliable. This application [holds up a piece of paper] shows a teen with excellent Apple and Windows operating system skills. It seems she (or he) has done some website programming, too! This other application [holds up a piece of paper] shows a teen who's only used Apple programming. Neither one has any previous job experience except baby-sitting and a paper route.

Ms. Not Likely: [As Ms. Not Likely approaches, Ms. Boss arises and extends her hand] Good afternoon, Ms. Not Likely.

Not Likely: [Gets up, stretches, saunters into the office, and sits, slumping and not making eye contact, ignoring Ms. Boss's outstretched hand, and mumbles] Uh-huh.

[Ms. Boss lets her hand drop, stands up, and turns to the audience. Not Likely "freezes."]

Boss: Well, what do you think? I'm inclined to skip this one entirely! [Elicits comments on the various negatives, then resumes her seat] Ms. Not Likely, it says here [picks up a piece of paper] that you have experience with Windows and Apple computers. That would be a real help at McInfo. How good are you at basic data processing?

Not Likely: [Staring at ground, mutters something]

Boss: Excuse me?

Not Likely: Uh, I said, uh, y'know, I'm okay at it. I guess. [Chews gum loudly]

Boss: So, you can type pretty well?

Not Likely: I guess. It's not typing, it's keyboarding. Doncha know anything?

Boss: [Gets up, turns to audience as Not Likely freezes] What do you think? [Encourage comments, including speaking clearly and being polite. If possible, make a distinction among humility, bragging, and the very necessary self-promotion required to make a good impression. The Boss sits back down.]

Boss: [Looks at piece of paper] You did some baby-sitting last summer, and I see you had a paper route in middle school. Do you have any other experience that would help you on this job?

Not Likely: Uh, no.

Boss: So, if we were to offer you this job, when could you start? It says here that you're 16. Do you need a work permit?

Not Likely: Uh, I dunno. I could start whenever. But I gotta have time for my gaming group (or team sport or whatever seems appropriate). And I can't work late on Fridays 'cause that's when I go out with my guy (or gal). How much does this pay, anyway?

Boss: Uh, thank you, Ms. Not Likely. That will be all. We'll be in touch. [Boss gets up to shake hands, but Not Likely just ignores it and shuffles off. Boss, shaking her head, turns to the audience. Ask them what they think about the last bit, and wind up with "I hope the next one will be better."]

Boss: Ms. Good Hire! [Boss arises and extends hand as Good Hire walks in] Good afternoon.

Good Hire: [Walks forward briskly, carrying her notebook. Takes the Boss's hand, shakes it firmly, and sits down. She sits up straight and looks right at the Boss.] Good afternoon, ma'am.

Boss: Ms. Good Hire, it says here [picks up a piece of paper] that you have experience with Apple computers. That would be some help at McInfo, but we also have machines that use Windows. Could you do basic data processing with Microsoft Excel or Word?

Good Hire: [Speaks clearly, looks Boss in the face] Well, ma'am, I'm very good using the Apple Mac at school for my projects there. I know I could pick up the Excel stuff really quickly.

Boss: So, you can type pretty well?

Good Hire: Yes, ma'am. I got a B+ in keyboarding.

Boss: [Looks at piece of paper] You did some baby-sitting last summer, and I see you had a paper route in middle school. Do you have any other experience that would help you on this job?

Good Hire: I think both those jobs are good preparation because I learned how to take on a project and get it done on time for my employers. One of the people I baby-sat for is on my list of references. [Good Hire leans over and points to the paper] They said I could use them for a reference. If you call them, they'll tell you that I work hard and follow directions pretty well.

Boss: So, if we were to offer you this job, when could you start? It says here that you're 16. Do you need a work permit?

Good Hire: I can start after next Wednesday. I can work every day except Saturdays. I don't have a work permit, though.

Boss: That's all right. We're not open on Saturdays, and McInfo can arrange the work permit for you. How about mornings from 10 A.M. to 2 P.M., Monday through Thursday?

Good Hire: [Opens notebook or day planner] I have to check with my parents, but I think I can do that. [Writes in notebook]

Boss: Uh, thank you, Ms. Good Hire. That will be all. We'll be in touch. [Boss gets up to shake hands, and Good Hire stands up with her and shakes] Good-bye.

Good Hire: Thank you. Good-bye. [Good Hire leaves]

The Boss gets up, turns to the audience, and asks them what they think. Have them contrast the two candidates, commenting on the "positives" of the second candidate. If they notice that Good Hire is less qualified (on paper) than Not Likely, so much the better.

Directions for Audience Participation

Props

- baseball cap, flip-flops, huge obnoxious jewelry (earrings, neck-lace, rings as appropriate to your sex)
- chewing gum
- a desk with a chair behind it and another chair in front of it

Have your audience imagine that behind the chair sits their future boss. (Point to the desk and chair set.) Ask them which behaviors are likely to get them hired or ignored by that boss. Act out the "negatives" and then turn and ask the audience what they think you ought to do instead. Demonstrate what they suggest where practical. See the Script for Teen Actors' Interview Skit for ideas of negative behavior, but be sure to cover the following:

- *Posture and demeanor*: Include sitting up straight, making eye contact, fidgeting, etc.
- *Clothing* (use the baseball cap, flip-flops, and jewelry): Ask the audience to point out good interview clothing from among the audience members or those on stage (i.e., you or the local businesswoman who is your guest speaker).
- *Language and attitude*: Include gum chewing, using titles (Ms. or Mr.), mumbling.
- *Preparedness*: Include sample interview questions and answers.

4

APRIL

This month's program is the busiest. As with the other programs in this book, much of the PR needs to have been done the month before, but it's especially true for this one. April is National Poetry Month, and what better intersection of interests—libraries, teens, and poetry—could exist? Programming for this month consists of two parts: a Young Writer's Poetry Contest, and a Young Writer's Coffeehouse.

Continue your Question Board with your own version of magnetic poetry. Thanks to the imaginative Angelina Benedetti of the Redmond (Washington) Library for this idea: Purchase a set of magnetic poetry words and a metal clipboard. Attach the clipboard to your Poetry Month bulletin board display or prop it up on your tabletop display of poetry books. Attach a selection of the magnetic poetry words (be sure to include plenty of connector words such as *the, I,* and *and*) so that there is enough space to manipulate the words to build short poems. A cheaper,

---

Begun in 1996 by the American Academy of Poets, National Poetry Month has swelled into a major happening. Visit the Academy's website at *http://www.poets.org* for free posters and information kits to help you celebrate poetry and the power of words with your teens.

disposable version can be made with paper. The same company that makes Post-it notes (3M) also makes double-stick removable tape. Print out a collection of words about 1" × 1" and 1" × 2" (*is* vs. *impressions*) onto index paper, or print onto ordinary paper and glue to index paper (see Figure 4.1). Attach the double-stick removable tape and tape the words to your Question Board with the headline "Instant poetry—just add words!"

Be sure to place your advertisements for the Poetry Contest next to the Question Board. You might add a small sign reading, "It's easy to make your own poetry; why not enter our contest?" I began doing the poetry contest over five years ago. The idea was written up in my library system's Young Adults' Librarians' monthly memo, "The Expletive Deleted Times," by the then Mercer Island Library's Young Adults' Librarian. I've modified, tweaked, and played around with the central idea but am forever grateful to her for a real winner. It consists of two parts: the contest and the celebratory coffeehouse to follow.

YOUNG WRITERS' COFFEEHOUSE WRITING CONTEST

I've always called my contest "(Name of Library) Young Writers' Coffeehouse Writing Contest" and encouraged not only poetry but also essays and short stories. I've even had one young teen ask if he could submit a comic strip series that commented on his middle school via a giant lobster. Of course, I agreed. If you wish to limit the contest strictly to poetry, then "(Your Library) Young Poets' Coffeehouse Poetry Contest" would be a more appropriate title. See Figure 4.2 for a sample flyer.

As you can see from the sample flyer, I invite teens in grades 7 through 12 to submit up to five entries that may include poems, short stories, or essays. The winning entries (including runners-up or honorable mentions) are invited to the poetry coffeehouse to receive their "honorarium" and to read their work aloud. See Figure 4.3 for a sample entry form. I usually judge the entries myself, but on a few occasions I've invited a member of the community to help me judge. The "honorarium" has always been a $10 prize awarded by my local Friends of the Library group to either the top two (middle school/high school) or top three (7th–8th/9th–10th/11th–12th) entries. If this is too expensive, small prizes or a certificate will suffice.

One special award, which I've always done and which costs very little, is to "publish" all the winning and honorable mention entries in a local

Figure 4.1
Poetry words

a	an	the	I	me	you
your	my	her	his	am	are
is	with	if	his	love	life

whisper	sing	howl
wild	troubled	dancing
dangerous	when	then
content	willing	impressions
desire	dangle	retreat
anew	before	within

Figure 4.2
Writing Contest flyer

(Name of Your Library)

Young Writers'
Coffeehouse

~WRITING CONTEST~

Read aloud your original writing!
Win prizes!
Be published in our Chapbook!

Grades 7 - 12 eligible

Entries may include a short story, an essay or a poem.
Limit 5 entries per person.
Final selections are made by the staff of the (Your Library)
and by volunteer judges from the (Your community).
Please turn in your entries to (Your Library).

Deadline to enter is (your date)

(Your Library's Name * Your Library's address *
Your library's phone number)

Figure 4.3
Writing Contest entry form

(Your Library's)
Young Writers' Coffeehouse
~WRITING CONTEST~
ENTRY FORM

RULES, GOOD IDEAS & HOW TO ENTER

1. This contest is open to students in grades 7 to 12.
2. Submit up to 5 entries, but use a new entry form for each one.
3. Submit a short story, an essay, or a poem.
4. Your entry should be clearly written and double-spaced. The judges will make no effort to understand sloppy or hard-to-read handwriting. Good spelling and grammar aren't *required* but we guarantee it will help.
5. We may be able to return originals to you, but we cannot guarantee this. Please keep a copy of your work.
6. Write your last name, first initial, the page number and the total number of pages on each page of your entry and attach it to this form.
7. You are preparing a piece to be read aloud at the Young Writers' Coffeehouse. A well-written but "R"-rated piece will unfortunately not get beyond "Runner Up" and is therefore not eligible to win a prize, although it will still be published in the chapbook.
8. Because you are preparing a piece to be read aloud, take the time to practice reading your writing aloud. Listen to how it sounds.
9. Featured writers (First place) will be awarded a $10 honorarium. If you cannot attend the Young Writers' Coffeehouse on Saturday, April 29th, from 6 to 8 pm (or Your date and time), an alternate from among the Runners-up will be featured in your place and will earn your honorarium. Your writing will still be published in the chapbook.
10. Turn in each entry to the (Your Library), attention (Your name), no later than (Your Library's closing time), Thursday, April 20th, 2000 (or Your date).

Name: _____ Grade: _____

Address: _____ Phone: _____

_____

I am submitting _____ Total pages: _____
TITLE OF THE SHORT STORY, POEM, OR ESSAY

chapbook. In one tiny community I usually publish *every* entry I receive! There are two ways to do this. The first and easiest is to use Microsoft Publisher™ or PageMaker or similar software, or a photocopy machine (reduce or enlarge as needed), to copy the entries onto letter-size paper. Use index paper or card stock for the cover, fold in half, staple with a long-handled stapler, and voila!—one chapbook. (See Figure 4.4 for detailed instructions.) Alternatively, ask teens who participated in your January bookmaking class to help you create a commemorative chapbook by using the bookbinding techniques outlined in Chapter 1. At a minimum you'll want to create one chapbook for your YA collection, although I usually create an extra chapbook for each participating school (i.e., if teens who attend that school are featured in the chapbook) and donate a copy to their school library.

Marketing for this program can take place in-house via displays and flyers and through announcements in your local paper. You might also want to send copies of your flyer to local coffeehouses. Depending on your community, this may be a big enough program to draw radio support. One of your best resources, however, will be the local high school and middle school teachers. Call to set up a meeting with the high school and middle school principals to outline this program to them. What they'll gain is a chance to reward their students for creative writing and support for any poetry or creative writing classes they offer. What you'll want is a chance to make a brief five-minute proposal at the next staff meeting asking English teachers to hand out entry forms or make them available to their students. If you've already established a good rapport with your local high school and middle school teachers and are comfortable booktalking, I can recommend a great tie-in booktalk (see following pages and "Olympic Poetry Script" section at the end of the chapter). At the least you'll want to mail a letter to each English teacher, school librarian, and school principal you serve, including copies of the flyer and entry forms. I have also found it *extremely* helpful to enlist the help of the school librarian so that the school library is also a place to pick up entry forms and turn in entries. This makes it much easier for teens who want to participate but find it difficult to get to the public library. See the sample letter in Figure 4.5.

Now's the time for your February program to really pay off. Contact all the teens who wanted to hear about upcoming library events. Give them a call or send them a letter with a copy of the entry flyer and entry form. Be sure to ask them if they'd like to volunteer to help out at the coffeehouse that follows the contest. Many teens now have to fulfill volunteer or community service hours as part of their high school gradua-

Figure 4.4
Chapbook Instructions

Use an 8½" x 11" paper set lengthwise (to "landscape", as many printers call it) and set the margins at ½" all around

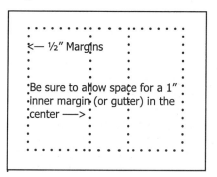

Type up or paste in the teens' entries

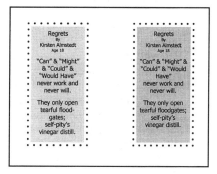

Use as many pages as you need to include all the entries. Doing some fiddly work with a good printer or running your pages through the copy machine twice gets you double-sided pages:

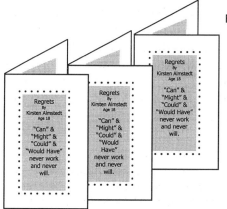

Fold these pages in half and insert into each other as shown, rather like a simple program folder. Take a final sheet of index paper or card stock, fold in half, and use for the cover. Either print directly on the heavier paper or onto a sheet of ordinary paper and glue onto the cover of your chapbook.

Use a long-handled stapler (available at many copy shops or purchase one for your library) to staple your book together.

tion requirements. It can't hurt to remind them that the library's teen programs provide a fun opportunity to meet that requirement. If you do use volunteers, take the time to debrief your helpers as you clean up after the program. Ask them what they thought worked (or didn't) about

Figure 4.5
Letter to schools promoting the Writing Contest

[Name of Teacher]
[School Name & Address]

[Date]

Dear Sir [or Ma'am]:

  This spring, schools and libraries across the nation will be celebrating National Poetry Month. [Name of your library] is no exception. I hope you will encourage your students to participate in our first annual Young Writers' Coffeehouse Writing Contest. Students may submit the poetry or short prose of their choice to [Name of your library]. Winners will not only be rewarded with prizes but will be invited as the guests of honor at the Young Writers' Coffeehouse at [Your library] on [Date of event], where they can read their work aloud. [Note: If you intend to produce a chapbook, add: "aloud, and will be published in the annual Coffeehouse chapbook."]

the program. Be sure to write these young people thank-you letters afterwards.

  Although I've written this as if the coffeehouse were an essential part of the program, it is possible to skip it if you're pressed for time and resources. The initial effort involved in setting up and doing this program is in designing the flyers and entry forms, writing reminder letters, making calls to teen volunteers and possible participants (those who responded positively to my February request about interest in library programs for teens), and setting up meetings with schoolteachers to promote

---

If you're comfortable booktalking and have a flair for the dramatic, try taking a variation on the poetry slam into classrooms. Visit *http://www.splab.org* for more information about nationwide poetry slams for teens and adults. I mix a variety of humorous, classic, story, and modern poetry into a 30-minute presentation I sometimes call Olympic Poetry. My teen audience not only listens to dramatic readings (and in some cases recitations from memory) of great poems but also gets to judge them as if I were taking part in the old Olympic Games when poems as well as athletics won the gold! For a full script see the Appendix at the end of the chapter. One caveat: If this poetry slam proves popular, you may be invited back next year and the year after and . . . ! I'm constantly on the scrounge for poetry that's fun to recite or read dramatically and has strong teen appeal. I also keep a folder where I stash lists of past poems (with notes on how well they were received) and new ideas.

the contest. The additional effort of poetry booktalks can make for a busy March and April. Much of March is used to promote the contest (including booktalks); the early part of April (usually the first two weeks) allows teens time to enter. I allow one week to judge the entries, mail the winners invitations to the coffeehouse (always follow up with a phone call reminder as if these were performers—actually, they are!), and have the coffeehouse at the very end of the month. Eliminating the coffeehouse would give you the whole of April for the contest. Even without the coffeehouse, being published in the chapbook is still a cool prize.

COFFEEHOUSE

On the other hand, the coffeehouse can be incredibly rewarding and fun. I've done a variation on it for teens for the past nine years and always have a blast. The teens, too, get a kick out of it—and it certainly makes great marketing for your library to that clientele in a way that parents and school officials are likely to appreciate. The opportunity to shine, to stand up and earn public approval for something they've done—when so often teens are in the spotlight for negative things—makes tying the coffeehouse into the writing contest a bonus for your teen clientele. This is another program that benefits from repetition and momentum as more teachers, parents, and teens enjoy the benefits.

Advertising for the coffeehouse, as mentioned earlier, relies on word of mouth among teens who have entered (and especially those who have won and will be presenting their work and receiving their prize) and on flyers sent to local schoolteachers and posted in the library. If your local paper permits (timing is sometimes tricky), you can write a press release that congratulates the winning teens and invites the community to the coffeehouse in their honor. See the sample coffeehouse flyer in Figure 4.6.

Other than advertising the event and writing and calling the participants, the coffeehouse is a fairly simple event to set up. Organizing it involves gathering the materials and setting up the space. Cover the

---

Is there a local writers group in your community? Do you know of any local authors? Invite them to your coffeehouse and add "Featuring—[Name of local author]" to your flyers. You'd be surprised at the positive response you can get!

Figure 4.6
Coffeehouse flyer

1st Annual
Young Writers'

Coffeehouse

Hear the winners of the writing contest read aloud
their original work! Read your own poetry or your
favorite poetry at our "open mike"!
Check out the published writing in the new chapbook!
All in a jazz-age coffeehouse atmosphere!

All ages may attend.

at [Your library]
[Your date]
[Your time]

Reasonable accommodation for individuals with disabilities will be provided.
Please contact the library prior to the event if you require accommodation.

library tables with colorful tablecloths if you have them handy; otherwise, use butcher paper and add a glass full of bright crayons. I'll usually snag fun poetry books from my 811s and 821s (including Jack Prelutsky and Shel Silverstein) to place on the tables, open or bookmarked to neat poems. Even old, jaded senior high students often have very fond memories of these humorous poets! Bring a tape player or boom box and borrow some mellow jazz from your library's music collection to set the mood. Arrange the tables so as to leave a space where presenters can read their poems. Add food and drinks (and of course, coffee), pull the shades or dim the lights, and your library meeting room is now the Teen Coffeehouse—at least for one night.

As teens, their parents, siblings, and friends begin to trickle in, greet them and encourage them to pick up munchies and drinks. About 15 minutes into the program, or when all the presenters have arrived, ask the audience to be seated. Tell them about National Poetry Month and the contest and chapbook. Introduce the winning poets and hand them their awards (check, certificate, or other small prize). Announce that the winners will share their poems with the audience. Tell them that once all the poems (or stories or essays) have been read the group will break for munchies and gather again for an "open mike" where everyone can have a turn reading their own poetry or sharing a favorite poem with the group. When each winner (including those who won honorable mention) has read his or her work, bring out the chapbooks, explaining that the winning writers' work will go into your library's Young Adult collection and a copy will be donated to the winning students' school library. Pass out the books for the audience to enjoy as they break for food and drinks.

When the group returns, you may need to jump-start the open mike portion of the program by reading or sharing a poem you like. Encourage the audience to draw from the poetry collections you've included on the tables or around the room. This is often the most dynamic portion of the event. In some cases, everyone is having so much fun they don't want to let me end the program and go home! If I have a guest speaker or presenter, I usually have him or her lead this portion of the coffeehouse.

If you've gone through the entire April program—including poetry booktalks, a writing contest, chapbook, and coffeehouse—you can relax a bit. Although you normally need to begin your PR and other preparations a month in advance, May is a minor exception. I've included some sample programs, but they're all optional. You'll be spending next month setting up for your summer reading program and your promotional presentations to the schools.

APPENDIX: OLYMPIC POETRY SCRIPT

[Introduce yourself and your library.] Before I begin, I'd like to find out how many of you have ever seen the Olympic Games. [Ask for a show of hands.] Did you know that long ago, during the very first Olympic Games, people could compete—and win—not only in sports like the marathon or wrestling, but in poetry? True! And some of those poems took as much as three days, from sun-up to sun-down, to recite!

In honor of National Poetry Month, [Our library] would like to bring you some Olympic-style poetry, where you get to be the judge. Later, you'll have a chance to be contestants yourself in the first annual Young Writers' Coffeehouse Poetry Contest. [Note: If you're only having the writing contest, it would be "Young Writers' Poetry Contest."] Who'd like to be a judge? [Wait for a show of hands, and pass out score pads to the judges.] I'll also need one person who's good with numbers to add up the scores—? [Wait for a volunteer, or enlist the teacher.]

Just as in the modern Olympics, you'll be giving every poem a score of 1 to 10. If a poem is so bad you can't believe someone killed a tree to write it down, hold up a "1." A "10," of course, is poetry ecstasy. Most poems, I know, are going to be somewhere in between. Don't hold back—if you think it stinks or shines, give it the score! But do try to give the poet a little credit and score the poem—not just my presentation.

[Pause. Let the silence grow a bit and then either read dramatically or declaim "The Ballad of Beth-Gelert" by William Robert Spencer.]

That was "The Ballad of Beth-Gelert" by William Robert Spencer. Judges, what do you think? [Allow for scores to be held up and recorded.] Notice that poem was also a story—based on the legend. If you visit Beddgelert in Wales, you can visit Spencer's dog's grave. A long time ago, back when the Olympic Games were still giving prizes for poems, any story that wasn't a history was considered "poetry." In truth, even "nonfiction"—great encyclopedias and histories—were done in rhyme with a distinct rhythm or meter. It was a part of the oral tradition—before the printing press and the mass production of books, the rhyme pattern and the meter helped people to remember. Of course, when you translate a poem from another language, you tend to lose both.

This next poem is from an unknown poet from Persia—what would later become Iran:

> He who knows not and knows not that he knows not, is a fool.
>   Shun him.
> He who knows not but knows that he knows not, is a child.
>   Teach him.
> He who knows, but knows not that he knows, is asleep. Wake
>   him.
> He who knows, and knows that he knows, is wise. Follow him.

Judges? What do you think of "He Who Knows"? [Allow time for scoring.]

Even after the oral tradition began to be replaced by the written one and books became common and novels were invented, poetry still held pride of place. Its special rhythm and meter and language were too important for everyday stuff. The stuff of poets was great histories, romances, love, and death.

[Pause. Let the silence grow a bit and then either read dramatically or declaim "Annabele Lee" by Edgar Allan Poe.]

Judges, what do you think of "Annabele Lee" by Edgar Allan Poe? [Wait for scores.] Pretty dramatic stuff, right? In a Mary Stewart novel, *Nine Coaches Waiting*, one of the characters claims that poetry is just "The right words in the right order at the right time." But that's a pretty big "just." Nonetheless, the way poetry can condense feelings and ideas so that your heart is stirred is pretty impressive. Certainly it stands up to the "important stuff" like love and death. Or freedom and justice.

Paul Laurence Dunbar, in the days of the civil rights movement, his heart torn with fury and despair at the injustice of segregation and hate toward blacks, wrote Sympathy (2) which contains the classic line: "I know Why the Caged Bird Sings." [Read or recite the poem and wait for scores.]

Injustice can burn the heart—and you don't have to be a great civil right leader or poet to feel it in your life. You can feel it when you're as young as 6 or 7 years old from the hands of adults who are supposed to care—but don't.

[Read dramatically or recite, "Purple" from *Step Lightly, Poems for the Journey*, edited by Nancy Willard.]

Judges, what do you think of Alexis Rotella's poem, "Purple"? [Wait for scores.] You can write about pride, too, with the same depth of feeling that Rotella and Dunbar gave to their poems about injustice, and maybe spark pride in someone else who's feeling ground down.

[Read dramatically "Phenomenal Woman" by Maya Angelou.]

That was "Phenomenal Woman" by Maya Angelou. Judges? [Wait for scores.] Poetry can tell a story, inspire an emotion, empower a people, and more. It can also be a joke or make you laugh. Here's one about an issue I know many of you can relate to:

[Read dramatically or recite "Homework, O Homework" from *The New Kid on the Block* by Jack Prelutsky.]

So what do you think about homework—I mean, the poem by Jack Prelutsky? [Wait for scores.]

Now let's find out who won. While we wait for the scorekeeper to add up the judges' scores, I'd like to pick up the score pads. [Gather the score pads from the judges.] Let's give a big hand for our brave and opinionated judges! [Wait for applause.]

[At this point in the program, while we're waiting for the score, I ask the entire class to explain what they loved or hated about specific poems. I pinpoint any of the poems that received a score of 3 or less or 8 or more. Was it the tumpty-tumpty rhythm? The drama? The lack of rhyme or meter? The idea expressed? If they could hear more poems, which ones would they like to hear more of?]

Is our scorekeeper finished? Yes? Thank you! A round of applause for our hard-working scorekeeper! [Wait for applause.] And the winner was [give name]. You can check out more of [name of winning poet]'s work at [name of your library].

There's a lot more to poetry—there are nature poems, experimental poems, poems with difficult forms like roundels, or spare and elegant ones like haiku. I hope you'll celebrate National Poetry Month with me and the [your library] by writing some poetry of your own. It can rhyme or not. It can have a rhythm or not. But write about what makes you angry, proud, or frightened. Capture a feeling or an idea that excites you. I'm looking forward to seeing your work! Thank you!

5

MAY

Although you can complete a year of Young Adult programs without doing any booktalks, because none of the programs described in this book specifically require them, this month is a bit different. The Who Wants to Win a Candy Bar trivia game is designed to include a few booktalks—you can leave them out, but your presentation will not be as effective. If you don't already have much of a relationship with your local schools, this is the month to press for it. You'll really want the opportunity to advertise your summer programs to these teens. Indeed, because visiting schools takes so much time away from the library building, doing any other programming is optional. This month you'll need to make calls to local businesses that you approached earlier in the year asking them to donate prizes for your summer reading program. I prefer to make the call, set up the meeting, and request the donation in person, but a letter can suffice. You'll find a sample letter in Figure 5.1.

This month's programs include a very simple Card Design project and a joint homeschool family program with your library's Children's Department. Of course, I realize that *you*, the librarian reading this, may very well be the children's librarian. If not, this is a sensitive departmental issue: Take the time to approach the children's librarian first, before you begin any planning for the event, and work with him or her.

Figure 5.1
Letter to local business requesting a donation

[Name of Owner or Manager—If you aren't sure, call!]
[Name of Business]
[Address & phone number]

[Date]

Dear [Owner or Manager],

   Earlier this year we met briefly and you said that you'd be willing to support the teen summer reading program at [Name of your library]. I was so pleased, because our new teen program needs community support and enthusiasm if we're to meet our goal. [Name of Library] wants our teens to see the library as a place where they belong (many stop using it around sixth grade) and to keep using its resources! We want, as I'm sure you do too, our teens to be enthusiastic readers and learners.
   As I mentioned when we spoke, the most valuable contribution is your time and presence in our teen programs, both as a role model and to reassure young people of their value to important members of the community. Nothing shows caring to children and teens like the time you make to be with them. In addition, we hope to provide incentives to teens this summer to read and to use the library resources. May I count on your business for a prize of [Make a suggestion: a $10 gift certificate or a prize in-kind—a bag of candy bars from a grocery store, a graphic novel or a game booster pack from a comic or game store, etc.] or whatever you think would be an appealing incentive?
   If you have any questions or concerns, please contact me at the above phone number, e-mail account, or address [or list them here if you aren't using letterhead stationery]. I'm available at [your library hours where it is easiest to reach you in person or by phone].

[Note that you must follow this letter up with a phone call, requesting confirmation of the specific prize and when you can pick it up. Be sure to write a thank-you letter immediately on receipt.]

When you create publicity for your summer reading program, it's nice to be able to have something splashy and eye-catching. But not everyone has a professional graphic designer on his or her staff. There is a shortcut, however, that you can take. Visit *http://www.publishers.org/home/index.htm*, the website of the Association of American Publishers, and click on the link to the "Get Caught Reading Toolkit." Although it's designed for publishers, it's easy to adapt for an in-house display.

CARD DESIGN PROJECT

Advertising for the Card Design project can be done by tying in with your Question Board. If you plan to have the project coincide with Mother's Day, post the question "What do you like best—or what would you change (if you could!)—about your mom?" Otherwise, set up a display of sample cards—easy to staple to a bulletin board or set up on top of a table—and a display of books on stamping or card making. Try asking on your Question Board, "What's the best kind of art?" Include a flyer for this program in the letters you send to schoolteachers telling them about the upcoming summer programs for teens.

The program itself requires one material outlay: the purchase of an attractive or unusual rubber stamp and gold or silver stamp pad. Look in the local Yellow Pages for a store that supplies a wide mix of stamps, or order via the Internet. Kidstamps, a stamp company that is popular with schoolteachers and librarians, can be reached at 212–291–6884. Card stock or index paper for the card, various colored papers and scraps, colored markers, and glue are all that's needed. A hand-made, layered card can be very attractive and relatively simple to create. Demonstrate the process, using a sample, and then turn the materials and supplies over to the participants. See Figure 5.2 for detailed instructions.

LIBRARY TRIVIA PROGRAM

I first got the idea for this trivia game after seeing it demonstrated by the talented Rochelle Brown of the Covington Library in Washington State. Each year I created a different script with different trivia questions and booktalks to match the theme of my library's summer reading program. This past year I decided to run a spinoff of the wildly popular game show *Who Wants to Be a Millionaire* called Who Wants to Win a Candy Bar (All of the suspense! All of the pointless trivia questions! And *none* of the money!). At the end of this chapter, you'll find a script, trivia questions, and even sample booktalks (which I've used successfully in the past) that tie in loosely with the programs outlined in the next chapters. I've included a few notes about modifying the game to include the Who Wants to Win a Candy Bar scenario. You can use it verbatim or take it as a template and adapt it to your local situation. The Library Lotto game mentioned in the full script is explained in detail in Chapter 6.

With middle schools and junior high schools, it's usually best to call

Figure 5.2
Card Design project

Tools Needed: Scissors, rulers, glue sticks, pencils, markers,
                         stamp and gold or silver stamp pad
Materials Needed: Lightweight, dark-colored paper
                         Contrasting colored paper scraps or lace doilies
                         8½" index or card stock (any color), cut in half

Arrange materials together on a side table and the tools on a table where the participants will be working.

Instructions: 1. Fold the card stock in half.

2. Use the ruler to measure ½" in on all sides of the front of the card.

 3. Use the markers to outline this border in a series of dots or dashes.

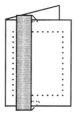 4. Cut a 1" strip of decorative paper, glue it, and "wrap" it around the front of the card, as shown.

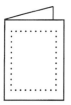 5. Stamp the gold or silver stamp onto the dark paper.

6. Cut away most of the dark paper around the image.

7. Cut out two circles of card stock smaller than the image.

8. Glue the circles together and attach them to the center of the card stock.

 9. Glue the image to the front of the card on top of the circles.

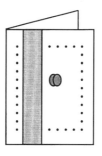

10. Color with markers as desired.

Having a "craft box" and maintaining a collection of snippets of interesting papers and other materials can pay off. Three years ago, I petitioned our Friends of the Library group to donate the money to purchase a core collection of tools, and I set aside one small filing cabinet to keep patterns, program notes, and assorted material supplies. It's been a real time-saver and gives me the flexibility of doing a low-key craft program when I'm pressed for ideas and time.

A good starter kit should contain:

- a large plastic tub for materials
- 10 staplers
- 10 tape dispensers and rolls of tape
- 10 scissors
- 10 glue guns and packages of glue
- 10 rulers
- boxes of glue sticks
- a set of magic markers or colored art pens
- boxes of pencils
- a ream of multicolored paper
- a ream of index paper or card stock

Save snippets of fancy papers, laces, doilies—anything that comes your way—and add them to your collection of materials. Turn to adult craft books for ideas. Generally, you know you have something that appeals to older teens if you can draw the adults in with your event as well.

the school librarian and set up a meeting with her. Explain that you want to promote the library's summer program for teens and encourage reading throughout the summer break. Ask if she can schedule library visits by you—usually two classes at a time works well—in her school library sometime in late May or early June. If she is willing to arrange this, it's a real bonus. Be sure to write a thank-you letter. Otherwise, offer to go class to class with your presentation (it takes 35 to 40 minutes). In the event that the school librarian is neither enthusiastic nor interested, call the principal to set up a meeting. Explain what you want and ask permission to individually contact the English, homeroom, or other "block" teachers to schedule classroom presentations.

With the younger teens of middle or junior high school, I simply play the game straight. It's a trivia contest set up like the television show *Jeopardy!* in which you read the "answers" and the students reply in the form of a question. The prize isn't money, but pieces of candy. The trivia questions and the "commercials" advertise library programs, the summer Library Lotto reading game, and library materials. I also bring samples of the Library Lotto lottery tickets (see Chapter 6, Figure 6.1) to hand out, one per student. The associated booktalks are geared toward that younger audience.

In the high school version, only the bookmarks and some of the trivia questions are changed. Although the game is simple (and silly), I find that by camping it up and playing the games for laughs the teens accept it and laugh along with me. Admittedly, it takes a willingness to be a bit silly in public. Older teens, like younger ones, are usually willing to be silly, but only if you are too. I'm not sure how well this approach would work for someone who is more comfortable making presentations in a calm, restrained fashion. If this is your style, it might be best to edit down the content to a very short (15 to 20-minute) statement about:

- who you are
- the materials the library has to offer teens, including magazines, videos, and so on
- the rewards of the summer reading program, Library Lotto (including sample lottery tickets to give to the teacher; let students know they can pick one up after class or at their teacher's discretion)
- a brief description of the summer programs, including an explanation of why you think the teens would enjoy participating
- one booktalk

You may want to offer this shorter, businesslike presentation to teachers who are seriously strapped for time at the end of the year. Even in high schools where I have successfully previously presented the longer, game format, time constraints have made it necessary to switch back to the shorter version.

You can also use the Library Trivia presentation as a program for homeschooling families. Check the Internet for lists of your state's homeschooling organizations. Many such organizations do regular mailings or have a newsletter for members. Send them a letter describing Library Jeopardy and the summer reading program for teens. (See Figure 5.3 for a sample.)

Normally it's necessary to prepare flyers and promotional materials up to four weeks ahead of time. So, as before, you'll need to be working

Figure 5.3
Letter to homeschool association

[Name of Local Organization]
[Address of Local Organization]

[Date]

Dear [Name of Local Homeschool Organization], [If you have a phone number, do call and ask the name of the person who acts as coordinator or group leader for this particular homeschool organization and use that instead.]

As you know, [Name of your local library] has always promoted and supported summer reading programs for children. We promote these reading incentive programs heavily at the end of the school year to local schools. This year, we're also trying to encourage teens to read [or to use the library]. As [Name of your position], I'll be coordinating the programs and publicity and wanted to invite your teenage students to attend, at [Name of your library], a program that we'll be offering to our local schools [Or use the name of high school or middle school, if there's only one.]

It's called "Library Jeopardy" [Or "Who Wants to Win a Candy Bar"] a gentle spoof of television game shows that challenges teen knowledge on a variety of subjects. The winners of these trivia games get small prizes [or candy] and we share information about the upcoming summer programs for teens at [Name of your library].

We hope you will share this information with your members and encourage them to attend. If you have any questions or concerns, please contact me at the above phone number, e-mail account or address [or list them here if you aren't using some form of letterhead stationery]. I'm available at [your library hours where it is easiest to get a hold of you in person or by phone].

Many high schools now have an additional reading requirement beyond what is assigned for classes. This extra requirement involves a certain number of pages, hours, or books. When you meet with the English teachers, try offering this addition to the traditional summer reading program: extra credit for summer reading. You will maintain a reading log at the checkout desk in which you record the student's name, school, grade, and the books he or she reads.

Because this setup can violate teens' privacy by revealing what they have read, the log should be kept behind the desk with prominent signs reading, "Ask for the Extra-Credit Summer Reading sign-up sheet at the front desk. Students in [Name(s) of participating high school(s)] only." It is also important to remind students, both on the sign-up log and during in-class presentations, that (1) the names of the books they read will (indeed, must) be shared with their English teachers in order for them to earn credit, and (2) participation is not mandatory. See Figure 5.4 for a sample reading log.

Figure 5.4
Reading log

(NAME[S] OF PARTICIPATING HIGH SCHOOL[S]'
EXTRA CREDIT READING LOG

Important! Signing the log indicates your permission for the library to share the information on it with (and only with) your high schools' English Department. Please keep this in mind when participating in the Extra Credit program. Participation is for extra credit and not required.

Your Name (please print)	Your signature	Grade this fall	High School you'll go to this fall	Title of Book	Author of Book	No. of pages

on the advertising for June this month. In addition, because the pro-motional material covers a summer reading program, you'll want to in-clude July and early August as well. It's more work, but as the children's librarians will tell you, it's worth it for the children's sake. I hope you'll agree that the extra time and effort are worth it for the teens as well.

APPENDIX A: LIBRARY JEOPARDY

Materials: Trivia question cards, trivia board with carrying strap (see Fig-ure 5.5), candy, "Vanna" attire (fancy floppy hat, feather boa, or large gaudy necklace), and sample Library Lotto entry forms.

Books: Blood and Chocolate, Ella Enchanted, The Hot Zone, I Am Jackie Chan, The Schernoff Discoveries, and Where the Heart Is.

Introduction

Good Morning (or afternoon), Ladies and Gentlemen. Ordinarily I work for [Name of your library], but for today [pause, use a dramatic voice] I'm [Your name], your host o-o-o-f LI-BRARY Jeopardy! I assume most of you are familiar with the TV trivia game in which I give the answers and you, the lucky contestants, give the questions? Before we begin, I'll need a volunteer from the audience. [boy or girl]

[Have the volunteer come up to the front of the room]. What's your name? [Wait for the answer.] The good news is that just for volunteering you win a prize. [Hand her a piece of candy.] The bad news is that you get to be my lovely assistant, [Volunteer's name], and wear the fah-boo hostess attire! [Place floppy hat, necklace, etc. on the volunteer and turn to audience.] Isn't she a dream! Let's have a big round of applause for [Name of volunteer]!

[Turn to your assistant.] [Name of volunteer], your mission is to hand out these fabulous prizes [raise bag of candy] to each winning contestant! [Turn to audience.] So who'd like to be a contestant on [dramatic pause]: LI-I-I-brary Jeopardy?

[When a teen raises his or her hand to volunteer, ask his or her name. Then say:] So [Name of contestant], what category do you choose? And for how many points? Remember! Answer in the form of a question.

Responses to Contestants

Your contestants will usually reply in the form, "I'll take 'Summer' for 200 points." You will then pull the trivia question card from behind the

Figure 5.5
Building a trivia board

Although I originally purchased something quite similar for about $55 from a teacher's supply store, this works just as well and is much cheaper!

Tools: Heavy scissors, pencil, ruler, glue, duct tape
Materials: Mat board (32" x 42") cut in half (32" x 21") of any dark color, white, unlined index cards (4" x 5"), strong, heavy ribbon or cord (4 ft.), complementary colored paper, contact paper

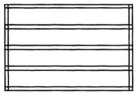

1. Measure and mark 1" in on all sides of the mat board.
2. Measure and mark horizontally, from the first 1" line at the top, 4" down, 1" down, 4" down, and so on until you reach the bottom.
3. Measure and mark vertically, from the first 1" line at the left, 5" across, 3½" across, 5" across, 3" across, 5" across and 3½" across, and 5" across.

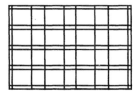

4. Use the duct tape to attach the index cards to the 4" x 5" squares penciled on the board. Note the open top. These will be the sleeves into which you can insert the trivia questions.

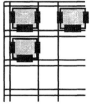

5. Cut out the colored paper to a size which will cover each index card plus the duct tape, and glue into place.
6. Label 4 each of the index cards "100", "200", and "300".

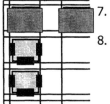

7. Glue a blank row of index cards across the top.

8. Glue the labeled index cards in rows of 100, 200 and 300 onto the center of each colored paper square until you have a grid:

100	100	100	100
200	200	200	200
300	300	300	300

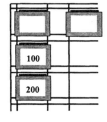

9. Cut strips of contact paper 4½" wide by 32" long and cover each row. Along the blank row this provides a surface to which you can attach and remove different "categories". Along the numbered rows, the contact paper keeps the board neat. Be careful not to block the tops of the sleeves.

10. Attach the cord or strong ribbon to the board with duct tape as shown.

game board and read the "answer" aloud. Your contestant gets first try to give the correct "question." If teens from the audience call out the answer, smile and say, "Only [Name of first contestant] gets to answer. If you're right, he's just won another round!"

If he gets the question right, have your volunteer take him a piece of candy (the volunteer may need prompting). Then let the contestant choose to go again. He gets to keep choosing and having first try at answering until he either gets it wrong or fails to answer in the form of a question. If either of these occur, turn the question out to the audience. The first hand to go up gets to try, remembering to "answer in the form of a question" until someone gets it right. That person becomes the next contestant, and play proceeds.

Booktalks and Other Commercials

In between "rounds," or when the teen draws the "Library Daily Double—You get two pieces of candy!" interject these brief spiels. Generally, I describe the Lottery game three times, tell about three upcoming programs, and do three booktalks for an hour program. Obviously, you can tighten this up by simply describing one of each and limiting the trivia questions to only one or two categories. I find it's helpful to be able to offer teachers on a tight schedule an abbreviated version of the promotion.

"We interrupt this program to bring you a special announcement of an upcoming Library Program. On [Date of program] at [Time of program], [Name of program] will take place. [Brief description of what the program is about and why it's cool.] It's free! It's fun! It's all for teens at the Library! [Pause and in a calm tone of voice add] We now return to your regularly scheduled programming."

Or—

"It's time for station identification! You're listening to *me* [Your name], host of Library Jeopardy, with my lovable assistant, [Name of volunteer]. This program is brought to you by [Your library], which wants you to have a great summer. Visit [Name of Library], where you can play Library Lotto, the only lottery where all it costs to play is what you're willing to read. Don't miss Library Lotto this summer at [Name of Library], where you can win, win, win!"

Or—

"Coming soon, to a library near you! Great books, great magazines, great reads! Just like: [Insert booktalk itself here]. Don't forget—for every book, magazine, or graphic novel you read, you can enter the Library Lotto game at [Name of your library] this summer!"

In the following titles, an asterisk (*) indicates a title appropriate for middle school as well as high school.

Blood and Chocolate by Annette Curtis Klause

Vivian Gandillon knows she's hot. She's tall, golden-tan, with long golden-blonde hair. She's smart and strong and sexy. Vivian's a werewolf. She loves what she is, loves the night and the hunt. She loves the powerful and painful magic of the change. All the boys in her pack howl after her. Yeah, she's hot and she knows it.

But Vivian wants more than animal lust. She wants sensitivity, respect, and tenderness. Vivian thinks she's found it in Aiden, a handsome poet in her English class. Even though he's a human, Vivian thinks he's special enough to understand her wild magic, strong and loving enough not to betray her secret to the human world that hates and fears her kind. But can a predator truly love her prey?

Then someone in her pack starts to murder people in Virginia, and Vivian begins to doubt. She's torn between human love and wolfish loyalty. It's hard to know which tastes sweeter anymore—blood or chocolate.

Read *Blood and Chocolate* by Annette Curtis Klause. It's a *really* different kind of love story.

*Ella Enchanted** by Gail Carson Levine

I'm sure you're all familiar with the story of Cinderella? [Pause as audience members call out the key points—the evil stepsister, the fairy godmother, Prince Charming, etc.] Well, this [Hold up the book] is Cinderella with a twist! *This* Cinderella's fairy godmother doesn't wave her wand and fix everything for Ella, oh no. *This* fairy godmother is the source of her problems! You see, when Ella was just a helpless baby her fairy godmother gave her the gift of perfect obedience. Sounds fine, right? "Hey Ella, put your toys away and take a nap," and without any fuss or whining, Ella obeys. Fine if you've got a loving mom and dad—maybe!

But this is Cinderella, right? Her loving mom is dead and she's got the wicked step-mother and equally nasty step-sister. And they've just discovered Ella's little problem. She has to obey any order, no matter what it is or who gives it to her. It's pretty bad.

How do you get your guy when you just can't say No? Find out in *Ella Enchanted* by Gail Carson Levine.

The Hot Zone* by Richard Preston

It's a major hospital in downtown Zaire. Charles staggers into the emergency ward. He's clearly very, very sick. Within minutes he's on a gurney and wheeled into the Intensive Care Unit. Dr. Musoke hurries to examine the man.

[Begin reading at "Dr. Musoke felt for a pulse" on page 18. Continue until "Dr. Musoke stayed by his bedside the whole time" on page 20.]

Within a week Dr. Musoke has the same disease and dies just as messily. Charles and the doctor both have Ebola Zaire, the deadliest virus on Earth. And this book, *The Hot Zone*, tells the true story of how this deadly virus came to the United States in a shipment of monkeys and nearly broke out in the suburbs of Renton, Virginia. That's right. It's a true story. Stephen King says it's "the scariest story he's ever read."

I Am Jackie Chan: My Life In Action* by Jackie Chan and Jeff Yang

How many of you know who Jackie Chan is? [Wait for responses. If no one volunteers that Chan is a movie actor who does his own stunts, offer that information.] But those stunts are just as dangerous as they look! [Open the book to the appendix listing his injuries.] In the course of filming, he's [Read the list of injuries].

And Jackie's life is just as wild as one of his movies. He was turned over to the Chinese Opera House in Hong Kong when he was only 6 years old. Until he was 18 they virtually owned him. They taught him all the skills he has—the gymnastics, the martial arts, and the acting—and he learned them perfectly. Unlike you, when he didn't do his homework his teachers were allowed to beat him up!

His whole life has been one weird adventure. Read about it in *I Am Jackie Chan*, by journalist Jeff Yang and Jackie Chan himself!

The Schernoff Discoveries* by Gary Paulsen

Gary and his buddy, Harold Schernoff, are the despised geeks of their high school. The jocks hate them; Julie Hanson, the hottest girl in high school, doesn't know they exist; and Gary would be failing if his genius buddy, Harold, didn't help him out. Harold also provides the spark that makes high school bearable. Take that time in chemistry class—[Read from "But I know what time it happened" on pages 6–9.] I've learned the sequence by heart so that I can just "tell" it, but it works to simply read the end of Chapter 1.

Read the rest of their adventures in *The Schernoff Discoveries* by Gary Paulsen.

Where the Heart Is by Billie Letts

Novalee has a kind of superstition about the number 7. She hates and fears it. She knows it means trouble. Maybe she has reason to hang on to superstitions; she sure doesn't have much else. She's got no home, no family that cares about her, she's seven months pregnant and heading out with her boyfriend, Willie Jack, from a small East Coast town to Bakersfield, California. He says he's got a bright new future ahead. Novalee dreams about a pretty home of her own for her, Willie Jack, and the baby.

Then Novalee asks to stop at a Wal-Mart just off the freeway in Nowhere Ville—Sequoyah, Oklahoma—to use the toilet, and she buys a magazine and gets back $7.77 in change. She knows it's a disaster. She's right. Willie Jack has driven off and left her, alone and pregnant, in a Wal-Mart in Oklahoma with nothing but the clothes on her back and $7.77. Her future looks pretty dark.

But when Novalee decides to hide out and live in the Wal-Mart— even has her baby there—her life takes a turn for the weird and the better. She discovers that the people in Sequoya can be strangely kind to a teenage pregnant girl. She discovers that having a home isn't so much about where you live, but who loves you. In the people of Sequoyah, at a small-town Wal-Mart, Novalee will find her heart.

She finds out that home is *Where the Heart Is*, a novel by Billie Letts.

Trivia Questions

Summer:

(100)   Your personal cost to rent videos, music CDs, books, magazines, and more from [Your Library] this summer. How much is nothing? Or, What is free?

(200)   This process of hand-dying cloth, similar to batik, was first popular in the 1960s "Summer of Love" but uses rubber bands instead of wax. What is tie-dye?

(300)   This summer you can [List some of your summer programs] and win prizes, all for free at this place. What is [Name of Your Library]?

Reading:

(100)   One of his most famous books is *The Cat in the Hat*. Who is Dr. Seuss?

(200)   You can star in an action film, blow up the school, be a werewolf, or die a bizarre death from Ebola Zaire with this. What is reading? Or, what is a book?

(300)   Once a year the best book for teens wins the Printz Award. The best book for kids wins this one. What is the Newbery Award?

Spectacular:

(100)   This spectacular form of body decoration dates back to prehistoric times. What is tattooing?

(200)   It took only two hours to sink, but this ship spawned the biggest grossing movie of 1998. What is the *Titanic*?

(300)   He's the biggest heart-throb, recording star, and action hero in Asia. Who is Jackie Chan?

Fun:

(100)   "May the Force be with you" was first said by what character? Who is Obi Wan Kenobi?

(200)   In this game you might be told, "Go directly to Jail." What is Monopoly?

(300)   The most popular comic book in the United States. What is The X-Men?

APPENDIX B: WHO WANTS TO WIN A CANDY BAR

Although the essentials remain the same (you need trivia questions, books to booktalk, and handouts for the summer reading program), this is slightly simpler, if slightly more expensive to perform than the Library Jeopardy game. The increased cost comes from needing quite a few candy bars in addition to the small bulk-wrapped candies. You also need many more pre-printed trivia cards (I used about 40 and should have had 60) and some objects to represent the "50/50," the "Poll the Audience," and "Phone a Friend" lifelines. The images in Figure 5.6 can be

Figure 5.6
Phone a Friend, Poll the Audience, and 50/50 lifeline icons

printed out, glued onto colored cardstock, and laminated with clear contact paper.

Introduction

How many of you watch TV? [Wait for responses.] O.K., so how many have seen the show *Who Wants to Be a Millionaire*? It's one of the most popular TV shows on Earth. There are copies of it in Greece, Belgium—even Russia has a version called *Oh Happy Man*! So [Your library] isn't going to be left out. We're bringing you our own version of the show. It has *all* of the suspense, *all* of the pointless trivia questions, and *none* of money! That's right! We're bringing you the premiere episode of [reach back and bring out a candy bar] Who Wants to Win a Candy Bar!

[Wait for snickers to subside.] I can just *see* the excitement rising in waves! [Pull out your list of about 10 to 15 trivia questions. Use the most recent edition of *The Guinness Book of World Records* and *World Almanac* for ideas. A sample question might be: What is the longest structure ever built by human hands? The answer is: the Great Wall of China.]

Our first contestant on Who Wants to Win a Candy Bar will be the first person to answer this question correctly." [Give the winner a piece of candy and bring her up to the front.]

As on the TV show, you get to choose among four possible answers to each question. Also like the TV show, you get three lifelines. You can use the 50/50 lifeline [Hand the teen the 50/50 icon] to cut the possible answers down to two. You can use the Poll the Audience lifeline [Hand the teen the question mark icon] and I'll ask your classmates to raise their hands if they think answer (a) or (b) or (c) or (d) is correct. You can use the Phone a Friend lifeline [Hand the teen the telephone icon] to ask any person in this room, including your teacher, to help you answer the question. Now. Are you ready to play Who Wants to Win a Candy Bar?"

Responses to Contestants

For every correct question, the contestant gets one small piece of candy. He or she only gets to keep the first candy—all others are forfeit if he or she gets the answer wrong. The teen can decide to walk away with all the small candies at any point before the next question is asked. Ham it up, asking, "Are you sure you want to risk it all? You have four pieces of candy and only one lifeline left!" as you play. Ask, "Is that your final answer?" at the end of every other response.

If the teen gets seven questions in a row correct, he or she wins the candy bar. Ham it up, asking, "Are you sure you want to risk it all? You have six pieces of candy and only one [or two, or three, or none, as appropriate] lifeline left!"

Trivia Questions

I had a mix of easy and hard questions, but I didn't try to increase the difficulty as the teens went along. A sample easy question was: The Heimlich Maneuver is used in: (a) Ice-skating, (b) Surgery, (c) Choking rescue, or (d) Getting a date. A hard question was: The most popular beverage of the ancient Egyptians was: (a) Milk, (b) Water, (c) Fruit juice, or (d) Beer. The tricky answer is, of course, beer.

6

JUNE

June's program is the Library Lotto game, which actually extends throughout the summer, as well as weekly displays to market the library collection. The additional programming is optional. If you decide not to include the additional events, your presentations to the teen students would only mention library materials (books, videos, magazines, CDs) and the Library Lotto game. Those presentations can extend through the end of May into June depending on the number of high schools, junior high schools, and middle schools in your district. If you haven't been gathering prizes throughout the year, or if the prizes don't seem appealing enough, you'll need to step up your efforts this month. Continue to contact those local businesses from which you got positive responses in earlier months. Set aside one decent prize for later—for September's Internet Scavenger Hunt.

A sample calendar for the summer reading program could follow a schedule of weeks one through six. Ideally, a full-scale summer program for teens would have one program every week, tying in to weekly displays of library materials and the weekly drawing of a Library Lotto winner. In times and places where I've been strapped for time, however, one program every other week (one in June, two in July, and one in August) seems to work fine, too.

LIBRARY LOTTO

The idea behind Library Lotto—which has been used in one form or another for nearly a decade by the Young Adults Services librarians of the King County Library System—is that reading or otherwise making use of library materials enables the participant to enter in a weekly drawing for prizes. The game mechanics are quite simple: Teens fill out an entry slip with their name, contact information, and a brief opinion about a book they've read, a CD they've listened to, or even a library program they've attended. Each entry form is like a lottery ticket, giving teens a chance to win a prize. As with any lottery, the more often they enter, the better their chance of winning.

There are two ways to use this program depending on your goals as a youth services specialist. Is it to retain the interest of young library users who seem to abandon public libraries in early adolescence? Or is it to encourage extracurricular reading and to regain the trust of teens who have come to view reading as a chore, forced on them by the demands of their schoolwork?

If your goal is the former, you'll want to focus on library materials and programming. Your Library Lotto ticket should read, "Play and Win! Check out any library materials or attend any library program and tell us what you think! Your brief review on this ticket enters you in our weekly prize drawing." You could, if time and money permit, collect and "publish" the best reviews in an end-of-summer newsletter. This approach, focusing on library use, including *all* media, proves more popular with teens who might not be drawn to a reading program per se. It tends, however, to be less popular with high school teachers and parents who usually prefer that librarians focus on rewarding reading books.

To shift the focus, the ticket should read, "Read and Win! Read any item this summer—book, magazine, graphic novel, etc.—and tell us what you think. Your brief review on this ticket enters you in our weekly prize drawing." Again, if time permits, a collection of good reviews published in the fall would be fun. See Figure 6.1 for sample entry forms.

Each week you'll need to draw a winning ticket, contact that person, and award the prize. To increase publicity and appeal, if I'm able to have all or most of my programs on the same day I draw the winning ticket at the beginning of the program. "You could win, too" tends to be an inspiring statement when teens see a peer win.

To manage the process, I find it helpful to keep the winning ticket

Figure 6.1
Library Lotto ticket (front and back)

Library Lotto Ticket

Name: _____ Age: _____

Address: _____

Phone: _____ E-mail: _____

What you're reviewing (Book, library program, CD or video, etc.)

Title of what you're reviewing : _____

What did you think of it? (circle one) ☺ ☺ ☹

Review: _____

_____
(continue on back if you want)

Library Lotto Instructions

- Check out anything from the library—including one of our summer programs!
- Fill out this ticket with your name and at least one way we can contact you if you win (by mail, by phone, or by e-mail).
- Tell us what you thought of the program, book, CD, etc. with a short review.
- Drop this ticket off at [Name of your Library]. We'll pick a winner each week!

Your Library's Name * Address *

And phone number

Review (Continued): _____

_____

_____

_____

_____

Need a winning display idea for June and early July? If you have a display cabinet, showcase the available prizes inside. Add a simple poster to the display with the words, "Want to win this stuff? Teens 12–18 [or grades 7–12] ask at the checkout desk." For a bulletin board, eye-catching visuals such as photocopies of the prizes or representative color photographs from magazines can be stapled to the bulletin board with the same poster at the center.

tucked into an envelope by the circulation desk. Attached to it is a printed list of the available prizes. Although I do call the winning teens at the first available opportunity, I can't always be present when the winners come to collect their prizes. So I rely on other staff to check the winning teen's name against the tickets in the envelope, let the teen choose a prize from the box in the staff room (or out of the display cabinet—see sidebar), cross off the prize from the list attached to the envelope, and return the ticket to my in-box.

In addition to the PR you've been doing through the schools, a few other program pieces may prove helpful. These include some sort of poster advertising the basic elements of the program that may or may not include free events for teens. You'll want to pass out these posters to any local businesses that teens frequent, such as popular clothing stores, local eateries, music stores, video stores, and comic and game shops. Not sure which businesses are the most popular? Approach teen patrons in your library and ask them politely.

Another helpful program piece is a bookmark with the titles (and brief annotations) of fun items to check out at the library. Because I always include booktalks with my summer reading presentations to the schools, I use these bookmarks as lists of the titles I've presented. It helps staff to locate the books when teens come in to ask for them. But don't be limited to just books: Include a sampling of readily available fun stuff that will fit the scope of your program, whether it's CDs, videos of interest, or magazines and graphic novels. On the reverse of the bookmark, include a brief description of the contest rules as well as (if applicable) the times and dates of the summer program. See Figure 6.2 for a sample bookmark.

Let's say that you've decided to go all out with teen programming this summer. Great! Here are two programs to choose from for the end of June.

ANIMAL RESCUE PROGRAM

This program will require help from an animal rescue society. I've used the local Greyhound Rescue group (*www.halcyon.com/greyhnds/*), as

Figure 6.2
Library Lotto bookmark (front and back)

Library Lotto
Read `em and win!

Blood and Chocolate by Annette Curtis Klause. She's a werewolf, he's the human poet she loves, known to the rest of her pack as "dinner." She says it's true love, but can a predator ever truly love her prey?

Ella Enchanted by Gail Carson Levine. She's Cinderella with a twist: Her fairy godmother cursed her with the gift of perfect obedience. How do you trounce the wicked step-sister and win the prince when you just can't say "No"?

Check out the movie "Ever After" starring Drew Barrymore and hunky Dougray Scott. Cinderella was never this romantic...

The Hot Zone by Richard Preston. Ebola Zaire is the deadliest, ugliest virus around. Here's the true story of how it nearly broke out in Renton, Virginia. Stephen King says it's "the scariest story I've ever read".

Check out the movie "Outbreak" starring Dustin Hoffman and Rene Russo. What if the breakout in Renton, VA, had threatened the whole U.S.A.?

I am Jackie Chan by Jackie Chan & Jeff Yang. He's the action hero who does his own stunts with an injury-list a chapter long, and his life is as wild as his movies.

The Schernoff Discoveries by Gary Paulsen. From taking on the entire football team to self-electrocution (Hey, there's a chance to see Julie Hansson, naked-!), these two geeks make the misery of high school pretty entertaining.

Where the Heart Is by Billie Letts. Novalee Nation is 17, dead broke, pregnant, and stranded in a Wal-Mart in the middle of Oklahoma. She thinks her life has struck bottom, but in truth, it's just beginning to go right...

Check out the graphic novel **Strangers in Paradise: High School**, by Terry Moore. Two best friends (real girls, not spandex babes) deal with nightmare teachers, high school pain and abuse.

Library Lotto Instructions

- Check out anything from the library; including one of our summer programs!
- Get and fill out a ticket with your name and at least one way we can contact you if you win (by mail, by phone, or by e-mail).
- Tell us what you thought of the program, book, CD, etc. with a short review.
- Drop your ticket off at [Name of your Library]. We'll pick a winner each week!

Coming soon to (Your Library)
(Your library's address)
(Your Library's phone number)

(Your program date & time)
Meet the Greyhounds!
Meet the super jocks of the dog world: Ex-racer greyhounds! Sponsored by (Your Local Group)

(Your program date & time)
A New-Fashioned Ice Cream Social
Teens! Cool down and help out: Let the library staff know what you'd like in videos, CDs, magazines, books, and more.

(Your program date & time)
Spectacular Ts
Make your own wearable art: Bring any 100% cotton item (T-shirts, shorts or socks) to a free tie-dye program. Learn how to make classic tie-dye and more.

(Your program date & time)
Comics Extravaganza
Bring your own comics to shop & swap and meet with comic store owner (Name of local owner) to hear about the latest news and upcoming releases.

Reasonable accommodation for individuals with disabilities is available. Please contact the library prior to the event if you require accommodation.

Not sure about running an animal program yourself? Check out the website of the Humane Society of the United States at *http://www.hsus.org/*. Look for regional contact points and write to ask about having volunteers from local groups present an animal awareness program at your library. According to its website (*http://www.nahee.org*), the National Association for Humane and Environmental Education (NAHEE) believes in "fostering kindness toward people, animals, and the earth" and offers "humane education for the MTV generation." Links on their site for both teens and for teachers and parents provide ways to get involved which could be the nucleus for a teen program.

I'm the happy owner of a rescue dog. The Greyhound Project, Inc., is a national organization with links to groups around the United States, Canada, and Europe. Visit its website at *http://www.adopt-a-greyhound.org* to find your own local group. Because the dogs have a history of abuse and are truly unusual stars of the animal world (reaching top speeds of 45 mph), I found that doing a greyhound program tapped in to the natural activism of teenagers as well as their interest in the unusual. A typical greyhound program involves a group of dogs and their owners "meeting and greeting" the public, as they discuss the history, special characteristics and unusual qualities of ex-racing greyhounds. Local animal shelters and pet rescue groups, however, will also work well. In addition to crediting the group you work with in all your PR pieces, if you do the program indoors you'll need some type of caging (such as an exercise pen), which the groups will often supply, a source of water, and tarps. Duct-tape the tarps to the meeting room floor and keep a mop and pail handy for "accidents."

It's a nice idea to have tabletop displays that tie in with the programs you offer. For example, for a program on rescued dogs you could have fiction such as Peg Kehret's *Cages* (Minstrel Books, 1993) and Sheila Burnford's *The Incredible Journey* (Bantam, 1987), nonfiction about animal shelters and assorted dog breeds, plus a poster advertising the program. Any interesting realia—a statue of an appropriate dog breed, for example—would make a nice touch. Be sure to update your Question Board as well. "What's the best breed of dog?—And why?" makes a good conversation starter.

CONTAINER GARDENING

You could also offer a container gardening class. It's useful to check with your local cooperative extension office or master gardeners group (call local nurseries for contacts) to get assistance if you're not a gardener yourself. Alternatively, you could do what I did and find out about container gardening from library books and videos. Remember, few things are more convincing than personal testimony: "Before I read these books and watched these videos, I didn't know any more than you did. Now, look at me—I'm teaching a class!" I found moderate interest in this program among young gardeners. The materials you'll need include:

- inexpensive terra-cotta pots (I encourage teens to bring their own)
- potting mixture
- Osmocote or other delayed-action fertilizer
- paper towels
- tablespoons
- seedlings or seeds
- permanent black markers (optional)

If you plan on easy cleanup, see the note about duct tape and tarps in the previous discussion about animal rescue programs.

Set up tarps under and around the tables and cover the tabletops with newspaper. Dump piles of potting mix in the center of each table and surround the mix with seedlings or seed packets. Have a display container of gardening books and videos visible in the room. After welcoming the participants, explain the advantages and disadvantages of container gardening. (Advantages: mobility, ease of replacement; disadvantages: susceptibility to cold and drying out, and the container must be cleaned out with with a 5 percent bleach solution if you want to reuse it.) Encourage participants to plunge their hands into the soil mixture and feel it. Explain the contents of the soil mixture, and mention that if they plan to plant a lot of containers it's often cheaper to mix their own. Demonstrate the method of planting either the seedlings or seeds (be sure to add a measured amount of delayed-action fertilizer to the mixture), and then let the teens try it themselves. Once everyone has their seeds or seedlings planted, have them take their containers to an outdoor tap (or to a sink where you don't mind a certain amount of mud) and water well. Wipe the outside of the pots with paper towels, and encourage the teens to check out the books and videos. If you have the time and inclination, it can be fun to include permanent black markers and decorate the pots with simple geometric patterns.

As ever, you'll want to publicize—with in-house advertising and displays, letters to local papers, and flyers posted around the town. A tabletop display of gardening tools, pots, and colorful books will draw all eyes to your flyer advertising the upcoming program. If you've decided to make a combined booklist–program list bookmark, keep a small stack of these handy by any program display or advertising (see Chapter 1, Figure 1.3, for a way to attach a pocket holder to a bulletin board display). Teens don't always have the time or inclination to jot down the program information—this way, they can take it with them!

If you choose to begin summer programming in addition to the Library Lotto game in June, you'll be pretty busy. Don't forget that you'll need to be working on publicity and planning for July's programs as well.

7

JULY

Whether or not you decided to begin summer programs in June, you'll want to take advantage of the lazy July days with one or more of these three programs. Keep in mind that summer can be a tricky time for teen programming. Many teens have summer jobs; families leave town for long vacations; and the schools are no longer available for help with publicity. The first program, New-Fashioned Ice Cream Social, is designed to increase teen involvement. The second, Spectacular Tie-Dye, is simply fun and likely to draw teens to the library. The third, a teen pen-pal program, could actually be initiated at any time of the year but is an exceptionally low cost (in terms of time, resources, and money) activity. Marketing these programs to teens remains important, and I'll discuss some of the resources other than the schools themselves, of which most aren't in session over the summer.

NEW-FASHIONED ICE CREAM SOCIAL

It's not easy competing with summer jobs and warm days. If your summer climate is ideal or you live near a river, lake, or ocean, any outdoor activity is likely to take priority over visiting the library. In-

Figure 7.1
Ice Cream Social flyer

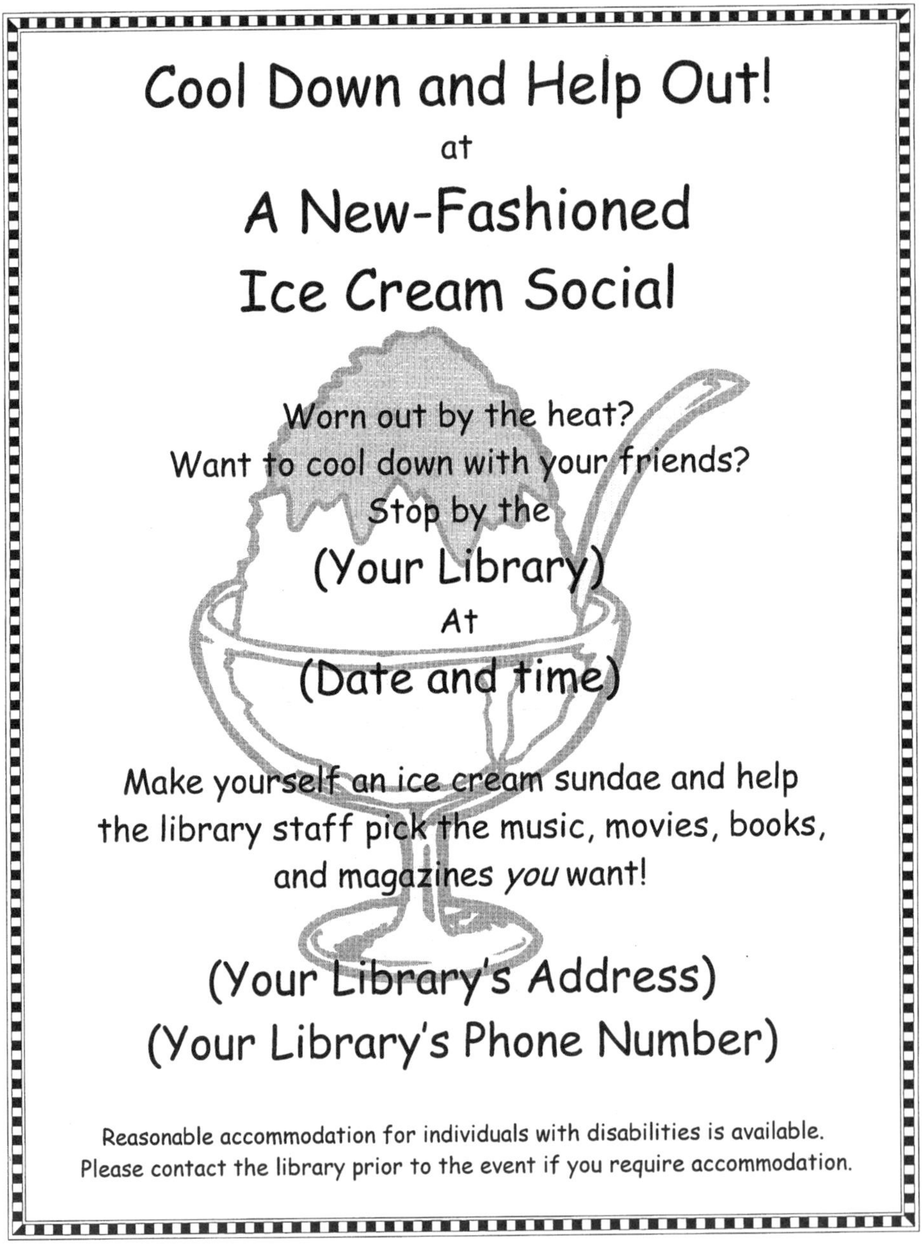

Cool Down and Help Out!

at

A New-Fashioned
Ice Cream Social

Worn out by the heat?
Want to cool down with your friends?
Stop by the
(Your Library)
At
(Date and time)

Make yourself an ice cream sundae and help
the library staff pick the music, movies, books,
and magazines *you* want!

(Your Library's Address)
(Your Library's Phone Number)

Reasonable accommodation for individuals with disabilities is available.
Please contact the library prior to the event if you require accommodation.

crease teen involvement and make the library more appealing on a hot day with a low-key focus group. In addition to a flyer announcing the activity (see Figure 7.1), you'll need:

- large paper cups
- plastic spoons
- a few cartons of vanilla, chocolate, and strawberry ice cream
- some maraschino cherries
- crushed nuts
- whipped cream in cans
- a tablecloth
- an easel with a flip chart
- a boom box or cassette player and music
- marking pens
- masking tape

Cover a table in the meeting room with the tablecloth and set up a "Make Your Own Sundae" bar. Have music playing on a boom box or cassette player. Set up a group of chairs in a circle around the easel with the flip chart, and once the participants have had a chance to make their sundae, ask them to gather around. Be sure to have multicolored marking pens and masking tape handy. (Now is a good time to draw the weekly winner in the Library Lotto program.) You'll be taking the part of facilitator for this focus group. Begin by assuring the group that there are no "bad" answers to the questions you'll be asking them about the library. Some may be better articulated or more useful, but all participation is helpful. Their input about library space, programs and materials for which teens are the primary clients will help make the library a better place for teens in their community. Write the key topic—one or two words only—at the top of each sheet of paper on your flip chart, and write down the key phrases of the teens' responses. If more than one teen proffers a suggestion, don't say "We've already got that," but praise the contribution and add a tick mark. Ask other teens if they agree, and add more ticks as appropriate. As each sheet gets filled up, tear it off and post it on the wall where it's readily visible.

Keep the focus relatively narrow, keep the experience short and sweet, and the teens will be glad to have participated. Here is a list of topics and questions for the focus groups to address:

- *The collection*: Keeping in mind what areas of the collection you can afford to expand, ask the teens what they've read, listened to, or watched recently. Did they like it? Did they get the media from the library? If not, why not?

- *The programs*: Have the teens attended any previous programs at the library? Why or why not? If they did attend, how did they hear about it? What did they like (or dislike) most about the program? If *they* could be in charge of programming for teens, what would they choose? Be careful to explain what these programs cost in terms of money and staff time, so that you don't raise false expectations.

- *The facility*: Whether your library's "teen area" is as small as one spinner rack of paperbacks or as large as an entire room, it's still helpful to get teen opinions. Do they use the teen area? Why or why not? If yes, how often? What do they like best about it? Least? If they could do just one thing (if money were no object) to the teen area, what would it be?

- *The library as a whole*: On a scale of 1 to 5, with 1 equaling really lousy and 5 nearly perfect, how do they rate: The library staff's helpfulness when they have a question? The library hours? How easy it is to get to the library? How often they find what they look for when they come?

Conclude by thanking teens for their help. Be sure to provide a means for them to see their involvement pay off. (For example, if there was a request for skateboarding magazines and your periodical purchase list is updated in October, you could add, say, *Transworld Skateboarding*. At that time, you'd make a sign reading "Coming in October: *Transworld Skateboarding*" and place it where the new magazine will be located.) After the program is over, post a short version of the focus group questions as the Ice Cream Social Survey (see Figure 7.2). at the reference desk and encourage other teens to fill it out throughout the summer.

One other point to consider with your focus group is timing it to happen before the arrival of a new collection. If money and space are available, link this focus group to next month's Comics & Cards Shop & Swap by adding a comic book and/or graphic novel collection to the YA section of your library. If you are able to do this, have the budget and the source (either a direct comic book distributor such as Diamond Comics—*www.diamondcomics.com*—or your local comic book store) identified ahead of time. Adjust the questions to primarily focus on the new collection: Do the teens read comics or graphic novels? If so, which are their favorites? Then, next month, use the Comics & Cards Shop & Swap to

Figure 7.2
Focus group survey

Ice Cream Social Survey

Teens! Please take a moment to fill out this short survey.
Your answers will help the library staff to serve you better.

Name: _____   Age: _____

When you come to the library do you generally find what you want? ❑ Yes   ❑ No

If no, what please give us a short list of what we're missing: _____

_____

_____

Please check the boxes if you think we're doing a BAD job with these collections:

❑ Science Fiction / Fantasy   ❑ Romance   ❑ Magazines
❑ Horror and thrillers   ❑ Mystery   ❑ Videos
❑ General fiction   ❑ Historical fiction   ❑ Music CDs/tapes
❑ Fun nonfiction books   ❑ Nonfiction for school ❑ Computers

If you checked any of the boxes, please give us a short list of things we could be doing better:

_____

_____

Have you attended any library programs? ❑ Yes   ❑ No

If yes, please list one program you attended: _____

How did you hear about it? _____

What did you like about it? _____

_____

What sort of programs would you like us to have? _____

_____

If you would like the library staff to contact you about upcoming events of interest to teens,

please give us your address or phone number: _____

_____

> Are you starting a new comic book or graphic novel collection from scratch? Don't miss Kat Kan's quarterly review of graphic novels in the *Voice of Youth Advocates (VOYA)*. Steven Weiner's classic guide, *100 Graphic Novels for Public Libraries* (Kitchen Sink Press, 1996), should also prove helpful. A good magazine source, which is slick enough to be popular with teens as well as a good source of information, is *Wizard Magazine*. Its website can be found at *http://store.yahoo.com/wizardworld/*.

showcase the new collection. Teens will be especially impressed at the results of their involvement: "Guess what? The library staff really does want my involvement and really did listen to me!"

Meanwhile, don't forget to update your Question Board: "What's the best (or the worst) thing about this library?" Change the tabletop displays every two weeks to tie in with the in-house flyers advertising the Ice Cream Social program. Set up a blender, appropriate dessert cups, and an empty ice cream carton (carefully washed out) and an ice cream scoop to capture the teens' attention and cause them to take a second look at the flyer. Ask library staff working at the checkout desk if they would, when a teen checks out materials, place a Library Lotto bookmark (see Chapter 6, Figure 6.2) in each teen's book, video, or CD.

SPECTACULAR T'S

This activity is fun and easy to do, but be sure to wear clothes you don't care about. Also, expect to have odd-colored hands for a few weeks afterwards! In addition to a flyer advertising the program (see Figure 7.3), you will need:

- Dylon cold-water dye in four attractive colors (I've found that dark purple, bright red, orange-yellow, and bright turquoise work well together.)
- four clean gallon jugs (I asked staff to bring in empty milk containers)
- salt
- a teaspoon measuring spoon
- a small funnel
- lots of rubber bands—at least 200
- at least 8 (but 12 is better) clear squirt bottles labeled with the colors of the dye you'll be using (Again, I asked staff to save

Figure 7.3
Tie-dye flyer

SPECTACULAR T-s!

(Your Library)
at
(Date and time)

Make your own wearable art: Bring any 100% cotton item: T-shirts, shorts or socks to a free tie-dye program. For Teens.

(Your Library's Address)
(Your Library's Phone Number)

Reasonable accommodation for individuals with disabilities is available. Please contact the library prior to the event if you require accommodation.

Figure 7.4
Tie-dye after-care instructions

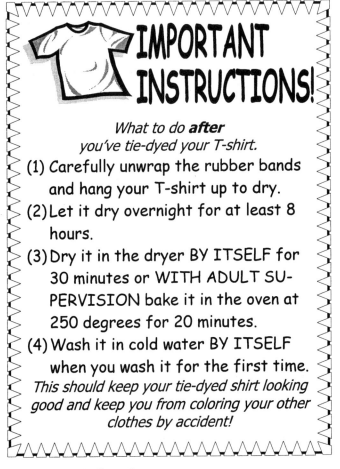

IMPORTANT INSTRUCTIONS!

*What to do **after**
you've tie-dyed your T-shirt.*

(1) Carefully unwrap the rubber bands
and hang your T-shirt up to dry.

(2) Let it dry overnight for at least 8
hours.

(3) Dry it in the dryer BY ITSELF for
30 minutes or WITH ADULT SU-
PERVISION bake it in the oven at
250 degrees for 20 minutes.

(4) Wash it in cold water BY ITSELF
when you wash it for the first time.

*This should keep your tie-dyed shirt looking
good and keep you from coloring your other
clothes by accident!*

Four sheets will fit on one 8½" × 11" paper

sports drink, bottled water, and soft drink containers; I also
bought a 6-pack myself.)

- at least 8 inexpensive aluminum pie tins
- a five-gallon bucket or plastic container filled with water
- plastic bags (I asked staff to save plastic grocery bags and the like
  until I had 40 or 50, but of course these may be purchased as
  well.)
- about 20 or 30 printouts of tie-dye after-care instructions (see Figure 7.4)

Expand your program options by tapping into local expertise: Try a program on tattooing and body piercing. Invite a local tattoo or body piercing artist to come to the library to talk to teens about this type of art. You'll want to use discretion and interview the tattooist or piercer ahead of time. Visit "Tattooing and Body Piercing: Decision Making for Teens" at *http:// www.vh.org/Patients/IHB/Derm/Tattoo/* for an excellent overview on the topic to learn what questions to ask. Yes, it's controversial. You'll probably want to make it clear that this is an informational program and that the library as an institution does not necessarily support piercing or tattoos per se. Nonetheless, this is information that many teens (and their parents) not only want but need. Facilitate this and you've got a great chance to show what libraries are all about!

A less controversial program topic is henna tattooing—in some cases it is possible to have a local artist actually tattoo the teens who participate, although you will probably only be able to get a demonstration for free or for a nominal fee. Because for some people henna tattoos have religious and cultural significance beyond mere ornamentation, it's a good idea to read up on the topic before approaching local artists. A little sensitivity goes a long way. "The Henna Page" at *http://www.hennapage.com/* is a good source.

- (optional) tarps, duct tape, and paper towels or rags
- Remember: Participants will need to bring their own T-shirts. If, however, you decide that your budget can stretch to providing the shirts, you can reduce the cost by purchasing men's 100% cotton undershirts.

Because I work in a large library system and this program is quite popular, I also bought a large plastic tub and extra dye and made it available as a kit to share with the other Young Adult librarians in my library system. You might want to save the supplies in a box, if space permits, and repeat the program three or four years down the road.

The basic idea is to demonstrate the various tie-dye wraps, including the standard starburst as well as a more unusual windowpane effect. The program is easiest to do outdoors, where you can spill or spatter dye harmlessly in the grass or on an asphalt parking lot. But if weather, safety, or some other factor is an issue, the activity can take place indoors. Use the duct tape to secure tarps onto the floor, being careful to cover it entirely. Wipe up spills with the paper towels or rags. I've done this three times indoors with no stains on floor or carpet—even after some blithe spirit poked holes into the bottoms of the squirt bottles!

About 30 minutes ahead of time, mix the dyes in the one-gallon jugs.

First, carefully put in the dye powder. Add about 2 inches of very warm tap water. Cap the jug and shake it well until the dye is dissolved. Next, add 4 tablespoons of salt and the packet of dye fixative that comes with the Dylon dye pack. Recap the jug and, again, shake it well until the salt and fixative are thoroughly mixed. Finally, add cool tap water until the jug is about one-half to two-thirds full—it's important to mix the dye quite strong, as the final color will be much lighter. Use the funnel to pour the dyes from the jugs into the appropriately labeled squirt bottles.

After preparing the dyes, set out the squirt bottles and the rest of the materials where the program will be held. Have the jugs of extra dye and the funnels handy to refill the squirt bottles as needed. Usually I place the bucket of water, the rubber bands, and the squirt bottles in the center of the space with the pie tins grouped around them. As the teens arrive, greet them and ask them to gather around the pie tins. Explain the procedure to them, and then turn them loose on the dyes. You'll want to move around the group, explaining the process to latecomers and lending a helping hand as needed.

The procedure is as follows. Have teens dunk their T-shirts (or other articles of clothing) into the bucket of water and wring them out thoroughly. Next, they should rubber-band the T-shirts in an interesting pattern. Two fun patters are the traditional starburst and a windowpane effect. The starburst pattern is achieved by finding the center of the design on the T-shirt and pinching it between the fingers. Using that center as a starting point, twist the T-shirt into a narrow tube. Tightly rubber-band the T-shirt at intervals down the tube. To get a windowpane effect, fold the T-shirt like a fan, with folds about one inch wide. Next, roll up the now-narrow T-shirt strip like a cinnamon roll such that you're left with a tight roll. Secure the T-shirt with rubber bands across the roll, rather like the sections of a pie. Whichever pattern they use, have the teens place their rubber-banded T-shirts in the aluminum pie tins and squirt them with dye from the squirt bottles. Be sure to soak each side of each shirt thoroughly with dye.

As the teens finish tie-dying their shirts, pass out the plastic bags and after-care instruction sheets. If you have helpful volunteers or plenty of time, you can staple the after-care instruction sheets to each plastic bag ahead of time; otherwise, hand them out together and keep reminding teens to take one home with them. If you're doing the program outdoors on a warm sunny day and have plenty of room, you could tie string to various sturdy objects about five feet off the ground and let the teens unwrap their shirts and hang them to dry. I don't recommend this, how-

Do you have a digital or Polaroid camera? If so, and if time permits, a fun way to advertise the continuing Library Lotto program is with a Gallery of Winners. When teens come in to collect their prizes, ask their permission to take and post their pictures. Under a banner reading "I won the Library Lotto!" post the photograph of the smiling winner. Instead of the person's name (for privacy reasons), post the name of the book (or other item) from the winning ticket.

ever, if the activity is taking place indoors or if space is limited. Instead, have the teens pop their T-shirts into the plastic bags as they finish.

To advertise the program, set up a display featuring a tie-dyed T-shirt, either pre-made (it's always a good idea to do a trial run of hands-on craft programs), purchased, or borrowed. You can staple it to a bulletin board with "Make This—Free!" strategically displayed, or you can use a coat hanger taped to any standard 8½" × 11" acrylic freestanding poster holder to make it the centerpiece of a table-top advertisement. Add 1960s period fiction such as Ruth Pennebaker's *Don't Think Twice* (Henry Holt, 1996) as well as craft and batik books. Continue to hand out Ice Cream Social Surveys to participating teens and to draw winners in the Library Lotto program.

Hang on to those survey questions and the notes from your Ice Cream Social program. In addition to providing marketing and planning information *right now*, they're invaluable tools for building a teen advisory board, or TAB. I'll discuss forming a TAB in more detail in Chapter 9.

Marketing your program in summer almost always involves doing without the very handy PR opportunities of your local schools. So aren't you glad you made those local contacts in February? Send flyers to local youth agencies: Boys and Girls Clubs, churches, local recreation centers, and, if you're familiar with them, teen hangouts such as local restaurants. Offer to post *their* flyers at the library. You'll want to continue to make phone calls or to send post cards to teens who responded positively during early surveys about being contacted about library events.

PEN-PAL PROGRAM

If you decided to only do the Library Lotto program last month, you're probably already stretched thin for staff time and money. The YA programming you've made a commitment to is a labor of extraordinary love. So, for an ultra low cost program, offer your teens the chance to travel for only the cost of a stamp—by making friends with a teen from another state. I manage the teen pen-pal program for the King Country Library System—a system truly committed to serving teens—so I have at-work time available to me to handle the applications from 50 branches. It only takes about one hour a week, plus an additional four to six hours a week for a month and a half when it's my turn to do the matching.

The impact of e-mail on the pen pal program has, in my experience, reduced the appeal of the program in wealthier King County suburbs where many teens own their own computers. Remember as well the factor that makes public libraries superior to the internet as the sole means of tracking down information (or, in this case, getting a writing buddy): librarians. We act as positive filters to gather reliable indexed materials and to help people find and use them. In our pen pal program, we help match particular teens from among the millions "out there."

You can be a part of this national pen-pal program. Diane Tuccillo of Mesa Public Library founded it over a decade ago. Your level of involvement is flexible: Choose to simply send your applications as they arrive to whichever participating librarian is handling the matches that month; or, if you are willing to commit the time and resources, volunteer to take a turn at handling the matching.

To get started, contact Kirsten Edwards, Pen-Pal Coordinator, King Country Library System, Duvall Library, P.O. Box 339, Duvall, WA 98019 (e-mail: kirstedw@kcls.org). The coordinator will assign your library an application form color (each state has its own, to facilitate matching teens) and determine your level of involvement. See Figure 7.5 for the correct form to use. Use this form and only this form, as the consistency of information about the teen applicants is important for the librarian matchers to do their job well. It is equally important to be consistent about the color of your forms and to *carefully examine* the information printed on them. Is it legible? Accurate? Type or rewrite the name, address, and zip code at the top of the page if any of these is *at all* unusual. What's clear to you may not be clear to other librarians across the United States or Canada. The program is limited to teens in grades 7 to 12 or between the ages of 12 and 18. If a child's application sneaks through, you'll need to return it to the child and explain that this is a teen program.

Every few weeks you'll receive a match list, that is, a list of pen pals for your teen applicants. Write them a letter letting them know about their new pen pal. A sample letter can be found within the spreadsheet instructions at the end of this chapter.

Make yourself a Teen Pen Pals notebook and a prominently labeled

Figure 7.5
Pen pal entry form

YOUNG ADULT
PEN-PAL
PROGRAM

Would you like to get to know another teen from a different part of the United States? Here is a chance to get into a "writeful relationship" with someone in Arizona, Ohio, or ?! The libraries involved will do the match-ups, and when enough people have signed up, you can begin a new friendship "write" away. We'd appreciate hearing how the communication develops after you get your new pen pal's name and address.

Fill out the attached form and return it to your local library to become part of this pen-pal program. The program is limited to teens in grades 7 to 12 or ages 12 to 18.

But PLEASE BE PATIENT! It may take 6 to 9 weeks to find the perfect pen pal for you.

(WRITE ON THE BACK IF YOU NEED MORE SPACE)

Date: _____

Name:_____ Boy ❑ Girl ❑ Age:____ Grade:____
     (PLEASE PRINT)

Address:_____ Phone: (____)_____
 (PLEASE PRINT) HOUSE NO.   STREET   CITY, STATE   ZIP

Interests & Hobbies:_____

Do you have pets? _____ What kind(s)?_____

School activities:_____

Books I like:_____

TV & movies I like:_____

Music I like:_____

Favorite famous people:_____

Career(s) I am considering:_____

Would you write often? ❑   or just occasionally?❑

How many sisters?_____ Ages?_____ How many brothers?_____ Ages?_____

Describe yourself in 25 words or less:_____

_____

RETURN TO YOUR LOCAL LIBRARY, ATTENTION: YOUNG ADULT DEPARTMENT

Your Library's Name * Address * Phone Number

Teen Pen Pals folder where applications can be placed as they arrive. From the pen-pal program coordinator you'll receive a list of librarians who are doing the matching during certain times of the year. Place this in your notebook. I recommend keeping the match lists for about a year in case questions arise. I also have a page where I keep track of the number of pen-pal applications I've received and the number of match letters I've sent out, and a pocket where I tuck the master disk I use to keep track of the pen-pal applications and their status.

Although it's possible to keep track of this with a card file system, I don't recommend it. The first time a helpful person tips out all 600 cards onto the floor, you'll have a deep appreciation of one of the reasons why. Another reason is that it adds quite a bit to the time and labor. The detailed instructions for setting up the pen-pal spreadsheet, including a sample spreadsheet, and for handling the process (including doing matching yourself) can be found in the following pages. The initial cost in time to set it up is more than made up for in the ease of handling and tracking applications afterwards.

To publicize your new pen-pal program, post flyers around town, contact the local paper, and make application forms available to local teens. The pen-pal application form (Figure 7.5) can also do double duty as a flyer.

Remember that the PR for each month's program needs to be done in the previous month. Don't forget to keep gathering prizes and to stay in touch with your local teens.

APPENDIX: PEN-PAL SPREADSHEET AND COORDINATOR INSTRUCTIONS

Spreadsheet

Create a spreadsheet with the fields shown in Figure 7.6. The reason for having fields for the applicant's name, address, and phone number are self-evident. The sex of the applicant is tracked because not all names are obviously male or female (and some, such as Kevin, can be deceptive: I personally know both male and female Kevins). If any of your teen participants have a question about the sex of their pen pal (and they often do), it's nice to be able to answer promptly. Age and deletion date are recorded because young men and women over age 18 are no longer eligible to participate. I track the dates of when forms are received and

Figure 7.6
Spreadsheet sample

Name	Sex	Address	Phone	Age	Date Form Rec'd	Date Form Sent	Date Matched	Errors, Notes Delete Date
Alpha, Jane	F	123 Any street, My Town, WA 12345	123-456-7890	12	Unknown	1-Sep-96	?	Sep 03 Del
Beta, Joe	M	123 Any street, My Town, WA 12345	123-456-7890	13	19-Apr-00	19-Apr-00	?	Mar 06 Del Called - waiting on good address
Gamma, Jane	F	123 Any street, My Town, WA 12345	123-456-7890	17	Unknown	14-Mar-98	15-Jul-98	Mar 03 Del
Delta, Jane	F	123 Any street, My Town, WA 12345	123-456-7890	12	13-Jul-99	13-Jul-99	12-Aug-99	Jul 06 Del

sent because I want to know just how long it takes to get a pen pal through this system and to be able to quickly catch any anomalies.

Set the formatting in the cells such that each cell's data will wrap. How you center the text, what size it is, and what font you use are up to you. If you're comfortable with some of the more esoteric spreadsheet and word-processing linkages, you can even use your spreadsheet to generate address labels. Use your spreadsheet's sorting functions to alphabetize the list.

Pen-Pal Coordinator Instructions

When the _____ (your library's color) forms are turned in

1. If not on the proper color paper, see "Other Notes" for instructions.
2. Note the date the pen-pal form arrived on the form.
3. File in a Pen Pals Folder: Filled Out Forms. Once a week prepare the forms.
4. To prepare the forms:
    a. Using Publisher or Word's label maker, print out the teen's name and address onto a label and affix on the form (usually in the graphics area). This makes it much easier for the librarian who is trying to read the address of areas he or she may not be familiar with.
    b. In bold marker, add near the label the letters for your library. This will help the matcher identify your library's participants.
5. Mail the forms to whoever is scheduled to do the matches. (Keep the list at the front of your Pen Pals notebook.)
6. Make or check the record: Load the Microsoft Excel (or other spreadsheet) file: Pen Pals-Database.xls which you have created and for every form you've prepared, check to see if the teen already has an entry.
7. If the teen already has an entry, update each applicable field: Age, if older (Field E), Date the form arrived (F), Date the form was sent to matcher (G), and Date the match letter was sent (H), such that each entry wraps neatly under the one previous. You may need to add five to eight spaces between each one so that they wrap neatly.
8. If the teen doesn't already have an entry, create one: Protocol for creating entries follows:

    a. Field A (Name): Enter the teen's name, last name first.

    b. Field B (Sex): Enter "M" for male or "F" for female.

    c. Field C (Address): Enter the address such that the street address is on one line and the city on the next within the box. You may need to add spaces for this to wrap properly.

    d. Field D (Phone): Type in the phone number with area code. Use the format: aaa-bbb-cccc.

    e. Field E (Age): Type in the age, then calculate in what year the teen will be 19 and no longer eligible to participate. Tab over to Field I (Errors, Notes, Deletion Date) and add a deletion note. Example: If "Mary" is 17 on March 15, 1999, when her form arrives by March 2001 she'll be 19 and ineligible: "Mar 01 Del"

    f. Field F (Date the form arrived): Type in the date.

    g. Field G (Date the form was sent to matcher): Type in the date.

    h. Field H (Date the match letter was sent): Type in a "?"

    i. Field I (Errors, Notes, Deletion Date): In addition to the deletion date (see Field E), use this space to note any problems that may arise.

9. When all the new applicants have been entered, choose "Sort" from the Data menu (topmost toolbar) and click on "OK." Sort alphabetically by last name.

10. Save one copy to the master disk, one copy to hard (C:) drive.

11. Note the number of forms sent out in the page of your Pen Pals notebook where you record statistics.

When the match lists arrive

1. Load the Microsoft Excel (or your spreadsheet) file: PenPals-Database.xls from the master disk.

2. For each name from your library on the match list, update the name in the spreadsheet.

    a. Field H (Date the match letter was sent): If adding a second (or third, etc.) entry, be sure to add it such that each date wraps neatly beneath the one above it. You may need to add five to eight spaces between each entry.

3. Save file to a master disk (A:) and to hard (C:) drive.

4. Create a form letter and fill it out as shown in Figure 7.7.

5. Place in an envelope with your library's return address, and mail.

6. When all the letters have been sent, note the information in the statistics section of your Pen Pals notebook, and file in the "Current Match Lists" section. Eventually, you'll want to toss old match lists to make more room.

7. Occasionally you'll have letters returned to you. First, double-check that you haven't made errors addressing the envelope, then try phoning the participant. If that doesn't work, simply file in your notebook under "Problems": The participant may contact you. After a year, it's safe to dispose of it.

When you're the matcher

1. You are responsible for matching, but contact Kirsten Edwards (the Pen Pal program coordinator) if you want to talk about how to do match-ups.

2. Some quick suggestions: Have a pizza party with a group of your best teen volunteers twice a month to do matches. Do it yourself every other week.

Other Notes

1. Although technically you're supposed to recopy all the information from the wrong color paper onto a fresh form of the correct color, here's a shortcut: Using ⅓ of a piece of plain paper of the correct color, staple it to the top of the form. When it comes time to attach the label with the neatly printed name/ address of the applicant to the form, attach it to this sheet.

2. Cell formats: Here's the formatting currently used:

   a. All fields have center vertical alignment.

   b. All fields have Ariel size 10 font.

   c. All fields have the "wrap text" box checked.

   d. Field A (Name) has Left (indent) "0" horizontal alignment.

   e. Fields C (Address) and I (Notes) have Left (indent) "1" horizontal alignment.

   f. Fields D (Phone), E (Age), F (Forms arrived), G (Forms sent), and H (Match letter sent) have Center horizontal alignment.

3. Use the Statistics section of the "Current Data Book" to record monthly statistics. In the past, pen-pal coordinators have

Figure 7.7
Match letter

Your Library's Name
<u>Your Library's Address * Phone Number (s)</u>

Dear: *(Name of Your Library's Pen Pal applicant)*

You recently requested a pen pal through your community library.
Here's good news! We have matched you up with:

(Name of person from the list with whom they're matched)
(Complete Address of matched person)

Why not write to your new friend right away?

We would like to hear how things are going, so when you have a chance, drop us a note in care of your local library.

We hope you have lots of fun getting to know your pen pal.

Sincerely,

(Your name)

Young Adult Department

counted the Pen Pal program as a program under their monthly Service Statistics report—adding up the numbers for each month's attendance figures.

4. Every so often it's a good idea to send word out to all the other participants in your library or library system that (a) you're the one doing Pen Pals, and (b) they need to use the correct color forms. Make master pen pal forms and basic instructions available to your staff.

5. A master disk with the form in Microsoft Publisher can be found in a slot on the "Blank Masters" file in your general Pen Pals hanging file.

6. The master disk for the Pen Pal database can be kept in the slot so labeled of your Pen Pals notebook.

8

◇◇◇ ◇◇◇ ◇◇◇

AUGUST

It's August, and your summer program is winding down. Even if you opted out of any other program but the Library Lotto for these months, it's time to wrap it up, recap your successes and failures, and think about what you want to do next summer. You'll be awarding the last prizes from your Library Lotto drawing and running the final event. Which events worked best? Why? Review the results from the teen survey and focus group in July. Knowing just how much work it is (though the rewards are worth it), decide how much time, energy, and money you can invest next year. Jot down notes and ideas and set them aside for use next spring. August is also the month to gear up for the start of the school year and to prepare for fall booktalks.

COMICS & CARDS SHOP & SWAP

The summer's last program, a Comics & Cards Shop & Swap, requires very little work to set up. I've found that it requires momentum to get going. It works best after several years, particularly as a part of some larger event. If your library holds a regular end-of-summer fair or party for the kids, ask to have a spot in it. Alternatively, if your community has some form of summer celebration in August, you could hold the event in that venue.

The idea behind the shop and swap is to provide a pleasant, moderated setting in which teens can swap the cards and comics they have for the ones they want. This program will help teens realize that *"yes,* your local library *does* have what you want or can facilitate your getting it!" You'll need:

- a flyer that announces the program and mentions a medium of exchange (see Figure 8.1)
- a poster setting the "prices" (see Figure 8.2)
- tables and chairs for spreading out materials and making swaps
- drinks and munchies (if the setting is appropriate)

Popcorn or pretzels and instant lemonade are cheap and tasty. The added advantage to popcorn—especially if you use the pop-it-yourself microwavable variety—is that teens will follow their nose to your meeting room, even if they didn't originally intend to come to the program.

Although it is not strictly necessary, to broaden the appeal of the program you might want to invite a local comic book or trading card storeowner to speak at the event. I've been lucky in that the local owner I've worked with is the Eisner Award nominee for community service, Perry Plush of Zanadu Comics, but even if your local dealer isn't running for library sainthood, she or a staff member may well want to help out. It isn't just for the free PR: Most small business owners have fond memories of the role public libraries have played in their own lives and believe we're forces for good in the neighborhood. Be flexible, arranging your program schedule to mesh with theirs, and ask them to bring any freebies or samples to share that might appeal. Let them set the topic if they have one, but be ready to offer this popular standby: "What's new and exciting in comics and trading cards?"

If you're able to hold the program as part of a larger community event, be sure to round up teen volunteers to help. If you feel you've tapped out the ones who responded positively to the spring surveys, call your local Boy, Girl, or Explorer Scout leaders, or the equivalent in your community, and ask for help. You'll want to have staff helping to hand out Ice Cream Social Surveys as well as running the booth at the event. You'll also need tables and chairs that you can bring to the event, so identifying a staff member with a large car or truck is necessary. Bring plenty of

Figure 8.1
Shop & Swap flyer

Comics & Cards Shop & Swap

What do the X-men,
Pokemon & Magic the Gathering have in common?
They might be going home with you at the Comics & Cards Shop & Swap!

Bring your favorite comics, trading cards & media tie-ins to

(Your Library)
at (Your date and time)
to swap with other collectors.

(Name of local comic store owner) will be there at (your time)
with free samples and sneak previews of upcoming comic and trading card sensations!

Reasonable accomodations for individuals with disabilities will be provided.
Please contact the Library prior to the event if you require accommodation.

(Your library's address) * (Phone number)

Figure 8.2
Shop & Swap price poster

Shop & Swap Prices

New comics	3 points
Old ratty comics	1 point
New paperbacks	5 points
Old paperbacks	1 point
Trading cards	3 points

ALL PRICES ARE NEGOTIABLE!

One company that has been particularly library-friendly is The Wizards of the Coast. This company makes popular trading card games such as Pokemon and Magic the Gathering and owns the Dungeons and Dragons company, TSR. Visit their website at *http://www.wizards.com* and check out the tournament information page.

Depending on the popularity of these games with your own teen clientele, you could offer the library space as a regular weekly site for gaming and trading (similar to a chess club—see Chapter 12, December, for more on that topic) or, better yet, run a tournament yourself. They're easy to set up, and the website has an abundance of information. You can also contact a local distributor for assistance—the website has links to help you find one.

library card applications and flyers for summer or fall programs, and be ready to talk up all the library has to offer teens in the community. If you have enough prizes to give away, use the February ballot (see Chapter 2, Figure 2.2) and strike out the sentence about guessing the number of candies. Have a prize drawing every hour or half hour.

The payoff in visibility for your program is great: You'll reach many teens who didn't believe or missed the message that your library now has great programs geared for them. On the other hand, because at the very least one library staff member will be away from the building during this event, there will be an element of stress for the rest of the staff. If your situation makes this an insurmountable problem, you simply may have to decide not to hold this event.

On the other hand, having your library staff regularly take part in a community summer festival or similar event is a generally good idea. Convincing your director or library board members may not be easy. Good ideas don't always get past individual personalities, and local conditions do vary. Ask yourself if you can be the spearhead to take part once a year at such an event. I've even tried (and it worked) offering to do the work gratis, on my own time as community service, if the library would back me with materials (tables and chairs, handouts, etc.) and preparation time. It pays off in the long run as the library institution and its staff are seen as fully participating members of the community at the most basic level. Such involvement also brings dividends during bond issues or intellectual-freedom challenges to a controversial but excellent Young Adult novel.

Consider this as well: Once you acquire the basic supplies for your booth, you can take it anywhere at very little notice. It transports easily to school cafeterias for lunch-break promotions of a new library program series or to state fairs or school career events. It's worth the time and

Even though this book focuses on low-cost, low–staff time programs, nothing is completely free in either time or money. Most of the best programs "cost" significant amounts of your time in making calls and personal contacts. However, I hope you'll consider trying to raise the money for some capital investments. One such investment, which has a fairly stiff start-up price, is a badge or button machine. Two online sources are Dr. Don's Buttons at *http://www.buttonsonline.com/* and Badge-A-Minit at *http://www.badge-a-minit.com/*. Both companies provide good-quality machines at a reasonable price as well as giving novel and inexpensive suggestions about how to use them in both programming and PR. The main appeal of a button maker, however, is in how much young people, teens especially, are drawn to it, so it makes a great eye-catcher at library booths.

effort to develop good-quality, long-lasting basic stock. Have a large sign (easy to read from a distance) with the library name and perhaps a slogan: "Books, Computers, and More!" Gather library card applications; prepare (if you don't already have one) a brochure with the library hours and contact numbers and an overview of special services of interest to teens, kids, and adults; and collect a few acrylic, metal, or cardboard stands for displaying flyers, brochures, and the like. Don't forget to keep a small stock of library freebies and handouts: attractive bookmarks, magnets, key chains, and so on.

In terms of marketing the program, even if you don't want to ask your local comic book or card dealer to be a speaker, do ask if you can post flyers in her store: It's a great way to reach your target audience. Of course, one of the best methods is to tie it in with your own library's comic book or graphic novel collection. If you don't have one, and you groaned at the thought of implementing one last month, think again. It's a popular medium, especially with teens, and like all media it encompasses both craftsmen and hacks. Some comics, such as Bryan Talbot's *The Tale of One Bad Rat* (Dark Horse Comics, 1995), rival the best in YA literature. One way to increase the likely involvement of a local comic book or game dealer in your program is to seek his or her help in setting up a collection. It's rarely cheaper to buy comics from distributors, so going local is not only convenient and flexible but also cost-effective. Change your Question Board to ask teens if they like comics or graphic novels and if so, which ones they think are the best.

Whatever you decide about your YA collection, use realia such as a popular comic book or card booster pack to draw attention to your flyers, and add to the display any graphic novels, comic strip collections (such as *Garfield* or *Mad Magazine* products), comic books, or books about these media that you already have in your collection.

Because you need to allow about four weeks for PR for any programs you do, this month will also include work on publicity for September. However, school will soon be starting again, and you'll be able to target your PR to one (or a few) central location.

9

SEPTEMBER

You'll be busy in September reconnecting with the local schools and preparing for school visits and booktalks. There will be back-to-school letters, meetings with school principals and English Department heads, and school PTA meetings. In light of this busy schedule, the first fall program is a low-key scavenger hunt. The game can be played either on-line, using the Internet, or (if your library's computer resources don't extend that far) with other library-based media. I'll also reprise the Book Discussion Group, because if you haven't begun one already, September is a great month to start laying the groundwork for one next January. I'll also briefly discuss turning that de facto Teen Advisory Board (what do you think you've been doing all summer with those volunteers and focus groups, after all?) into a regular and recognized library volunteer program.

INTERNET SCAVENGER HUNT

Get out that prize you set aside back in June, as you'll want it for the Internet Scavenger Hunt. Post it prominently, either on a tabletop display or with a facsimile (a photocopy or a magazine picture that approximates it) stapled to a bulletin board. Have the words "Test your Internet (or Searching) Savvy—and Win!" above it with the flyer (see Figure 9.1) advertising the program below. Have the entry forms (see Figure 9.2) placed near the tabletop display, or use the pocket pattern (see Chapter 1, Figure 1.3) to add them to a bulletin board. To really catch your clientele's attention, tape one of the narrow half-page flyers (see Figure 9.3) directly to each computer with Internet access.

The Internet Scavenger Hunt makes use of teens' natural competitiveness and curiosity in a positive way. Everyone has a chance to win, not only because the answers really are "out there" but because library staff are available (and prepared) to show them how to get the answers they want. It's a not-too-subtle piece of PR for teens and staff: Teens can find what they need to know at the library, the library staff are glad to make it easy, and—surprise!—it's a fun experience.

The penultimate piece of set-up for this program is involving the rest of the library staff. Post a flyer prominently with a note taped to it: "Dear Staff, teens will be asking for your help in solving these Internet puzzles—Go ahead and help them—It's not cheating! Just be sure to let the participants know that one of the easiest and best ways of getting an answer—whether surfing the Net or not—is to ask a librarian!" Be sure to take a minute to talk to all the staff who are expected to help patrons with reference questions and let them know about the program. You may want to post the answer sheet (see Figure 9.4) at the reference desk where staff can easily refer to it. It's important that the staff perceive this as a pleasant interlude through which their expertise can be shared easily and painlessly, so that the teens they work with come away with a positive attitude—and so that the teens themselves appear as interesting and pleasant clients to the reference staff.

Finally, designate a spot where completed entry forms can be turned in to you, and set a start and end date for the scavenger hunt. When the deadline arrives, check the answers. If more than one contestant found all the answers, or if there is some other tie, shuffle the entry forms and have another staff member draw a winner randomly. Contact the winning teen by phone, e-mail or letter and award the prize. For at least a week after the end of the program, post a list of the answers and place a sign across the picture of the prize (or the entry form, as appropriate) reading, "We've got the answers!" and the first names of the winning teens. If you have access to a Polaroid or digital camera, ask the winners if you can post their pictures as well. Although this won't do anything to boost your program's appeal this September, it will affect teens' per-

Figure 9.1
Scavenger Hunt flyer

[Your Library]'s
Teen
Internet Scavenger Hunt

[Your start to end date]

Test your surfing skills!
Win prizes!
Enter the Teen
Internet Scavenger Hunt
at [Your Library]
Today!*

*The Teen Internet Scavenger Hunt is open to teens in 7th to 12th grade and runs from [Your start to end dates]. Answers and winners will be announced on [Your date]. One entry per person, please. Turn in entries to [Your Library] on or before [Your end date].

First prize is [your prize], second and third prizes are [your prizes]. In the event that more than one person solves the hunt completely, the prizes will be awarded by a random drawing.

[Your Library]
[Address]
[Phone]

Figure 9.2
Scavenger Hunt entry form

[Your Library]'s Teen Internet Scavenger Hunt

The Teen Internet Scavenger Hunt is open to teens in 7th to 12th grade and runs from [Your start and end dates].

Answers and winners will be announced on [Your date]. One entry per person, please. Turn in entries to [Your

Library] on or before [your end date]. While teens may work in teams to solve the hunt, no adult is supposed to

assist the participants. First prize is [your prize], second and third prizes are [your prizes]. In the event that more

than one person solves the hunt completely, the prizes will be awarded by a random drawing.

Find out what you have to be to win the Michael L. Printz Award. _____

Find the location of the JWPT (Jersey Wildlife Protection Trust) and what it is. (Caution! This is a tricky

question!) _____

"What's All This About Wombats?" Find out why so many on-line librarians think they're cool.

_____

Bonus point: Find out who drew the picture of the wombat sitting on the computer terminal.

_____

Find out who killed Kait Arquette. _____

Find out when Teen Read Week is. _____

Where is Tunguska, and why should X-Files agents Scully and Mulder care? _____

_____

What's your first name and what does it mean? _____

How do you say "howdy" in Japanese? _____

Find out one piece of advice to give an Evil Overlord. _____

_____

Name 3 members of the Seattle Thunderbirds team. _____

_____

****

Your name: _____ Grade: _____

Your address or phone number, so we can contact you if you win: _____

_____

Figure 9.3
Scavenger Hunt half page flyer

[Your Library]'s
Teen
Internet
Scavenger Hunt

[Your start to end date]

Test your surfing skills!
Win prizes!
Enter the Teen
Internet
Scavenger Hunt
at
[Your Library]
Today!*

*The Teen Internet Scavenger Hunt is open to teens in 7th to 12th grade and runs from [Your start to end dates]. Answers and winners will be announced on [Your date]. One entry per person, please. Turn in entries to [Your Library] on or before [Your end date].

First prize is [your prize], second and third prizes are [your prize]. In the event that more than one person solves the hunt completely, the prizes will be awarded by a random drawing.

[Your Library]
[Address]
[Phone]

Two flyers will fit on one 8½" × 11" sheet of paper. Attach these flyers to library computers with Internet access and hand them out as bookmarks to teen patrons.

Figure 9.4
Scavenger Hunt answer sheet

Teen Internet Scavenger Hunt Staff Answer Sheet
Staff Information

- This program is open to students in grades 7–12 or age 12–18 only.
- Teens may work together to figure out the hunt, but no adults should assist them beyond the mechanics of how to get around on the Net. If, however, the teen has the savvy to ask at the reference desk, it's allowed to point the teen to the correct website. (After all, when you *really* want the answer, ask a librarian!)
- The program runs from [Your start–end dates]. No entries will be accepted after that date.
- The prizes include: [Your prizes]

Answers

- The Michael L. Printz Award goes for excellence in young adult literature. To win it you would have to be a Young Adult novel (or author). Website: *http://www.ala.org/yalsa/printz/*.
- The Jersey Wildlife Protection Trust (or Jersey Zoo) was founded by Gerald Durrell. "Jersey" refers to the Channel Islands of that name. The website is at *http://www.durrell.org/zoo/*.
- Wombats are the mascot of the reference librarians' listserv "Stumpers List." The how and why of wombats and librarians can be found at *http://www.cuis.edu/~stumpers/*.
- Bonus point: The artwork was created by Kirsten Anne Almstedt (now Edwards).
- Kait Arquette was the daughter of YA author Lois Duncan. The mystery of her death (no one is sure who killed her) and the intriguing history behind it was told in *Who Killed My Daughter?* (Dell, 1994). Up-to-date information can be found at the author's website: *http://www.iag.net/~barq/lois.html*.
- Teen Read Week is an annual celebration of teens, reading and libraries sponsored by YALSA, a division of the American Library Association. Its website (and scheduled dates) can be found at *http://www.ala.org/teenread/*.
- The official X-Files website at *http://www.thex-files.com/* explains the significance of Tunguska.
- The Behind the Names website at *http://behindthename.com/* is a fun way to find out more about first names and what they mean.
- Say Hello to the World (including Japan) at *http://www.ipl.org/youth/hello/*.
- The Evil Overlord website at *http://home.kscable.com/tung/overlord1.htm* contains literally hundreds of good ideas of what not to do.
- The Seattle Thunderbirds, like many sports teams in the United States, have an official website. Theirs can be found at *http://www.mcneel.com/users/Tbirds/*.

ceptions of their library as a place where they (or teens like them) can succeed and win.

As you'll notice in Figure 9.2, the sample entry form is designed to be used with Internet access. The answers to the questions can all be found on-line, and appropriate websites are identified on the answer sheet. Using search engines such as Google or Yahoo it's quite easy to track down the correct answer. That, by the way, is the point. The questions may seem obscure and the search will lead teens to some curious and interesting sites, but success is guaranteed if teens put forth a modicum of effort. To alter the format so that it uses library reference sources, or to change the questions, think first of the source you wish teens to refer to: for example, the dictionary. Next, phrase the question such that it gives a clue to the type of reference source: for example, "What does it mean to be a xenophile?" Build both challenge and success into your program design and you'll be right on target with young people who are stretching their wings but still need a safe spot to land.

An abbreviated form (three to five questions) can be used as an activity for class visits to the library. Because the population group is teens, I visit "the father of all novelty items"—the Archie McFee (available on-line at *http://www.archiemcphee.com/*) store—for cheap, zany prizes. When I can't afford to play to teens' real needs or wishes, I can play to their sense of the absurd. The response, even with sophisticated ninth graders, has been positive.

BOOK DISCUSSION GROUP

If you started a Teen Book Discussion group last January and suspended it over the summer, now is the time to get it going again. You could even bring copies of the Scavenger Hunt entry form to the first meeting. Refer to Chapter 1, Figures 1.6 and 1.7, for posters and bookmarks you can modify with fall and winter dates. You might add "We're back!" as a bright header. Enclose the flyers and bookmarks in your back-to-school letters (see Figure 9.5), set up in-house displays, and send press releases to the local newspapers. The Question Board might be modified to ask "What's your favorite book?" or "Are you looking forward to going back to school? Why or why not?"

If, on the other hand, you haven't started a book discussion group but, buoyed by the success of your teen programs throughout the year, you're looking ahead with an ambitious eye to next January, September is a good time to lay the groundwork. The outline for setting one up is given

Figure 9.5
Back-to-School letter

[Name of Teacher, School Librarian or Principal as appropriate]
[School Name and Address]

[Date]

Dear Sir [or Ma'am],

   Welcome back to a new school year. I hope you enjoyed your summer. At [Name of your library] we're gearing up for an exciting fall with new programs for young adults that we hope will appeal to your students [if writing to the school principal or school librarian, add "and to your teachers"]. Coming in September we have [Name of the program you hope to do, perhaps the Internet Scavenger Hunt], and in October we'll be celebrating Teen Read Week with [Name of your October program] and more.

   I also hope to [start or continue] a teen book discussion club and to continue to provide community service opportunities for local teens. [If applicable, "Our new Teen Advisory Board will provide them with a chance to assist their peers, the library staff, and our community by improving the quality of the library's Young Adult department and by assisting with library programs."]

   [For the school principal, you should request to be included in the first all-staff meeting. For the school librarian, if you're continuing or hoping to start a book discussion group based after school in her library, you should add a brief note requesting to meet with her on the subject. In both cases, be sure to follow up your letter with a phone call and a request for a meeting.]

   If you have any questions or concerns, please don't hesitate to contact me at [Name of your library] at [Your library's address, phone number, and, if applicable, your e-mail address]. I'm generally available at [Your shift dates and times].

Enc.: Flyers for [Name of your library]'s September teen program.

   [Note that with slight modifications this letter can also be sent to various home-school associations in your neighborhood or be published as an open letter in a homeschool newsletter.]

in Chapter 1. But whether you're planning for this book discussion group, or getting a Teen Advisory Board (TAB) started, or simply doing the Internet Scavenger Hunt, your first step is to become a part of the agenda of the school principal and the school librarian of the schools you serve.

   Although back-to-school letters are important, I want to stress the importance of making a phone call to set up a brief meeting with these people, as well as with (if applicable) the school's English Department head. Make the call, schedule a meeting, and at the meeting outline the programs you'll be offering teens not only this month but throughout the school year. Make it brief, a "heads up" about what you and your library have to offer their students this fall. Ask the school principal for ten minutes at the next all-staff meeting, and if you plan to start a TAB, ask which teachers would most appreciate being able to offer the local library as a community service opportunity. Ask the school librarian for cooperative program advertising, and if you hope to set it up that way, sound her out about cooperating on a book discussion club. In addition, mention to the school librarian that you're approaching the principal or English Department head as a courtesy as well—even if they don't respond.

Once you're at the staff meeting, keep it brief. If you asked for ten minutes, deliver your spiel in six and allow the remainder for questions and comments. It's the best way to ensure you can come back, if you want or need to. Because I enjoy and am good at booktalking, I usually begin by booktalking one adult novel with teen appeal. Visit the American Library Association's *Alex Award* website at *http://www.ala.org/yalsa/booklists/alex/* for a great list of titles. If you aren't comfortable booktalking, the phrase "It's my job to make yours easier—if I can" works to catch their attention.

Once you've got their attention, tell them what you can do for them and for their students, phrasing it in terms of their goals as teachers and educators. For example, if you're promoting your new Teen Advisory Board, you can tell the staff, "I know your students have a community service requirement. By joining the library's new Teen Advisory Board, they can serve their community by improving the library's service to their peers. I'll be working directly with the teens, and I'm happy to organize what you'll need for your school records." If you're starting the book discussion group, tell the staff, "Next January, to kick off the Michael Printz Award for excellence in Young Adult literature, we'll be starting a teen book discussion group. Your students who enjoy reading and literature will have a chance to share this pleasure with other students. We will reinforce the value of critical thinking and the appreciation of good literature that you're teaching in your classes."

Close your presentation by encouraging the staff to contact you when they are starting up large projects with their students so that you can put the resources of the public library at their disposal. Hand out flyers advertising the upcoming library programs, and ask them to share this information with their students or post them in their classrooms. Thank them for their time, and promise to keep in touch with them about future library events. Be sure to keep that promise.

> A closer look at library Teen Advisory Boards cross the country is available on the World Wide Web. Use the search terms "Teen Advisory Board" and "Library" to see what other youth-serving librarians are doing.
>
> The Arlington (Virginia) County Department of Libraries Teen Advisory Board showcases boards set in multiple locations: *http://www.co.arlington.va.us/lib/teen/tab.htm*.
>
> The Teen Advisory Board Page of the Appleton (Wisconsin) Public Library has links to the minutes of past meetings: *http://teen.apl.org/TAB/*.
>
> The Pasco County Library System in Florida has an interesting teen volunteer page at *http://power.pasco.lib.fl.us/teen_volunteer.html*.
>
> The Bay County Library in Michigan has a good application form online for their Teen Advisory Board. Check out their Teen Page at *http://www.baycountylibrary.org/TeenPage/teenboard.htm*.

TEEN ADVISORY BOARD

Chapter 1 detailed a sample Book Discussion Club meeting. Some of the basics, that is, having munchies and an icebreaker planned, apply to your Teen Advisory Board as well. One of the main differences is the agenda. For a book discussion group your role is to facilitate discussion—to talk just enough and be involved just enough to get the teens going on their own. As the leader of a group of volunteers, you will need to provide a more structured agenda for the monthly or bi-monthly meetings.

After allowing time to socialize and blow off steam, bring out those Ice Cream Social Surveys and your notes from the focus group program in July. Spread them out and talk about them. What consensus can you get about the library from the teens who participated? Brainstorm ideas and tasks for the advisory group and for the library's YA department (even if that department is only you in a semi-official capacity). Be sure to bring to the meeting a list of ongoing chores or long-term projects that members (and other teens whom they and you will recruit down the road) could perform without necessarily having to attend monthly meetings. Examples include processing chores for books, comic books, and magazines; creating a paperback book or comic book database; or starting a library newsletter. Ask for ideas for such projects from your TAB.

These teens will be your core group of advisors. They may stop by to volunteer an hour every week or two on ongoing projects, or they may pitch in on an "as needed" basis for special projects. But once a month, or every other month, you'll get together to assess how the volunteer work is going and to come up with new plans and new projects for the YA program at your library.

I will give you fair warning: Working with teens, especially idealistic young volunteers, isn't going to save you time. You aren't getting a handy new work force. Yes, you'll be able to take on projects for which two hands just aren't enough, and you may well be freed from some quotidian library tasks, but the reality is that you'll find yourself embarked on bigger, more challenging (and much more interesting) projects with your teens.

If you used September to take it a bit easy, that's just fine. As with April's Poetry Month extravaganza, there's plenty to do in September to prepare for the equally bustling month of October and for Teen Read Week. You may also discover as you read ahead that you want to do a full-scale Mystery Night program. It won't be too soon to start the groundwork now. I've tried to space the larger programs far enough apart to give you plenty of recovery time. Each year, when the fuss dies down, I half-swear I'm through. I think it's going to be low key and small scale for the rest of the year, and yet each year, after a month or two, I'm ready to fire it up again. I hope you'll find this is a workable strategy, too.

10

OCTOBER

October is the month to celebrate Teen Read Week. Teen Read Week was developed by the American Library Association and the Young Adult Library Services Association to encourage teens and the adults in their lives (parents, teachers, and librarians) not only to set aside time for reading, but also to develop a positive attitude toward this activity. As summed up by Carol Minnick Santa, the president of the International Reading Association, "Reading is a worthwhile life experience." This chapter suggests an easy book cover design contest and, for those with storytelling skills, a teen Urban Legend program, "Fact or Folklore?" As ever, I recommend booktalks, both as part of your library's PR and for their use in connecting teens with books. If there was ever a month where this connection deserves to be emphasized, October is it.

TEEN READ WEEK

The Teen Read Week book cover design contest originally came about as an annual "Save This Turkey" Thanksgiving program for older elementary school students. Each year, a few excellent (and sometimes out of print) titles with shopworn or uninteresting covers were proffered to

In March 1998 the librarians who participate on yalsa-bk, the Young Adult Library Services Association's listserv for discussing YA literature and concerns, were polled to come up with their all-time favorite books to share with teens via booktalking. Here are the highlights, books that two or more YA librarians considered their booktalking favorites:

- *The Face on the Milk Carton* (Bantam, 1990) and *The Terrorist* (Scholastic, 1997) by Caroline B. Cooney
- *Staying Fat for Sarah Byrnes* (Laurel Leaf, 1995) by Chris Crutcher
- *Don't Look Behind You* (Delacorte, 1989) and *Killing Mr. Griffin* (Bantam, Doubleday Dell, 1993) by Lois Duncan
- *The Ear, the Eye and the Arm* (Puffin, 1995) by Nancy Farmer
- *The Music of Dolphins* (Apple, 1998) by Karen Hesse
- *Downriver* (Atheneum, 1991) by Will Hobbs
- *The Silver Kiss* (Delacorte, 1990) by Annette Curtis Klause
- *Ella Enchanted* (Harper Trophy, 1998) by Gail Carson Levine
- *The Giver* (Houghten Mifflin, 1993) by Lois Lowry
- *Scorpions* (Harper Trophy, 1990) by Walter Dean Myers
- *Rats Saw God* (Aladdin Paperbacks, 1996) by Rob Thomas
- *Homecoming* (Atheneum, 1981) by Cynthia Voigt
- *Deathwatch* (Laurel Leaf, 1993) by Rob White

budding artists: Read the book, draw a cover design, and the best one will adorn the book cover from now on! It was mildly popular and connected a few kids with books they might not otherwise have checked out. Three years ago, however, Young Adult librarian Angelina Benedetti came up with her own book cover design contest that has proved appealing to young teens as well. I used it then, very successfully, as part of my first Teen Read Week program, and the following year it was adopted by nearly all the Young Adult librarians of the King County Library System. See Figure 10.1 for a sample Book Cover Design Contest entry form.

The program is easy to implement: Simply print out the entry forms and make them available to teens. During Teen Read Week, post the entries and offer visitors to the library a chance to vote on their favorite. I label each entry "Entry #1," and so on, to make it easier for teens to vote. It's nice if you have a small prize to award the winner, but in fact it's the chance to have one's work on display and admired that's the real reward. A sample ballot is shown in Figure 10.2.

PR for the program can be as basic as sending entry forms to local

Figure 10.1
Book Cover Design Contest entry form (front and back)

Teen Read Week Book Cover Contest
Show off your creative talents. Create a book cover for your favorite book or the book that you will write someday. This contest is limited to readers between the ages of 12–18 or in Grades 7–12.

Author Note
Here is where you tell us more about the author and other books he or she has written.

_____
_____
_____
_____
_____
_____

Entry #

Back Cover

Book Spine with the Book Title

Back Cover

Book Description
Give a brief description of the action, theme and main characters. Make your audience want to read it!

_____
_____
_____
_____
_____
_____
_____
_____
_____
_____
_____

Teen READ Week
[current slogan]
Design Your Own
Book Cover Contest

Here's How to Enter
1. Design your own book cover for a book you like or will one day write.
2. Write your name, phone number (or address), & age on this form & turn it in to a librarian at [Your library's name] by [Your program end date].
3. All entries will be displayed in the library. You might even win a prize!
4. Teen Read Week is sponsored by YALSA, a division of the American Library Association. This contest is sponsored by [Your Library] *
[Your Address & Phone Number]

This is the back side of the entry form and is designed to fit across a legal-sized piece of paper set to landscape (height at 8½" and length at 14").

high school art teachers, their school librarians, and the middle schools' homeroom teachers and school librarian. Or you can go all out and schedule promotional booktalks for the first week in October as well. Even some of the best books have bland covers—after promoting, say,

Figure 10.2
Book Cover Design Contest ballot

Name: _____

Contact me by: ❑ Phone   ❑ Letter   ❑ E-mail (please check one)

This is my phone number/address/e-mail address: _____

_____

Age or Grade: _____ School: _____

Do you want to be contacted about library programs for teens?   ❑ Yes   ❑ No

Which book cover do you like best? Entry Number _____

Three ballots should fit on one 8½" × 11" sheet of paper.

Richard Preston's *The Hot Zone* (Anchor, 1995), point out to your listeners that they may well have a better idea for a cover design—and a chance to prove it. At the same time, I excerpt stories such as "The Choking Doberman" from *The Big Book of Urban Legends* (Paradox Press, 1994) to promote the upcoming Urban Legends program at the library.

URBAN LEGENDS PROGRAM

The Urban Legends program, like booktalking, does require storytelling skills. If you're uncomfortable performing, this program may be easier and more appealing to you if you either hire a local storyteller (usually fairly inexpensive) or set it up to encourage audience participation. I have run the program myself as a "believe it or not" experience, drawing heavily on resources such as Julie Mooney's and the editors of Ripley's Entertainment's *The World of Ripley's Believe It or Not* (Black Dog & Leventhal, 1999) as well as the definitive source for distinguishing between the strange-but-true and the merely strange, the "Urban Legend Reference Pages" at *http://www.snopes.com/ulindex.htm*. These sources pro-

Do you need more ideas for publicizing and celebrating Teen Read Week at your library? Visit the official website at *http://www.ala.org/teenread/*. The American Library Association graphics department sells snazzy posters, bookmarks, T-shirts, and more that can be used in publicity and as prizes.

Are you looking for a good storyteller? The National Storytelling Association may be contacted at P.O. Box 309, Jonesborough, TN 37659 (800–525–4514, 9 A.M.–5P.M. ET). Their associated website at the National Storytelling Membership Association is located at *http://www.storynet.org/nsa/about-nsa.htm*.

vide a number of "legends" that, though bizarre, really happened. The storytelling skills come in structuring these real events into a very short and snappy story. Jan Bruvand's *The Big Book of Urban Legends*, Thomas Craughwell's *Alligators in Sewer: And 222 Other Urban Legends* (Black Dog & Leventhal, 1999), and Kristin Gilson's *The Baby-Sitter's Nightmare: Tales Too Scary to Be True* (HarperCollins, 1998) are all interesting sources for modern folklore, all handily crafted into short snappy stories to either tell (the preferred method) or read aloud dramatically.

You'll need a meeting room–sized space in which chairs can be set around a central "stage," and a whiteboard or flip chart on which to record audience "votes." If you have a microphone with which to mark out center stage (and amplify the voices), so much the better. It's possible to rent microphones overnight from party equipment and supply rental stores for a small fee. Begin by introducing the concept of the urban legend: a popular story that many people believe is true but that never really happened. Point out that it isn't so much the strangeness or the disgusting character of the story that makes it folklore, it's the fact that it isn't true and especially that it cannot be documented or traced. "It happened to a friend of my friend's ex-boyfriend" is one of the classic hallmarks of the urban legend.

Once you've set the stage and explained the concept, offer to share with the audience a handful of stories and ask them to judge whether the tales are "Fact or Folklore." After each story (and, we hope, some applause), ask the audience to vote on whether the incident described really occurred or is actually an urban legend. Record their votes on the whiteboard or flip chart. After telling approximately three of each (which will take between 20 and 30 minutes, including the time spent voting), go back over the votes, story by story, first noting whether or not the audience thought it to be a true story or an urban legend, then revealing whether or not the event actually occurred, and, if it is available (for those you pull from the "Urban Legends Reference Pages" site or from *The World of Ripley's Believe It or Not* it will be), some of the story's background.

Finally, ask members of the audience if they know any urban legends or stories that they're not sure are real or not. Invite them up to the microphone to share. Although teens are a fount of stories such as these, they're also worried about looking foolish in public. If you can, bring the microphone to the first volunteer and be very supportive. If the volunteer is unsure about the truth or falsity of her story, go back up to the whiteboard, erase the votes (or turn to a fresh sheet of paper on the flip chart), and write the address of the "Urban Legend Reference Pages" website. Let the audience know that they can visit this site and check out the information for themselves.

The less comfortable you are telling stories, or the larger your audience, the fewer stories you can tell. Therefore, a best-case scenario would be to tell one of each and have the teens' own stories take up the remainder of the program. Acting as the moderator, you might ask certain questions to encourage audience participation: What about your family? Did anyone you know ever see a ghost or have a weird experience that couldn't be explained? Do you think there are any local cover-ups? Do you know of any suspicious happenings that weren't (but should have been) investigated? Do you know of any place that's supposed to be haunted or where something strange happened that's particularly scary?

Be sure to keep an eye out for Evie Wilson Lingbloom's upcoming work on urban legends and folklore among modern teens. You should find it an invaluable tool if you decide to pursue this programming to any extent. Certainly, because an Urban Legends storytelling program involves teens, gives them a platform to be heard, and encourages them to seek out the truth for themselves, it could easily bear repetition every two to three years.

Of course, your PR for it will include flyers and letters to the schools. See Figure 10.3 for a sample flyer. When you write to the English teachers, be sure to point out the research and critical thinking skills this program will promote. In-house advertising can include a display of urban legend books, ghost story collections, and true crime novels. A tie-in for the Question Board is to print out one of the more bizarre stories from the "Urban Legends Reference Pages" site, tack it to the Board, and ask, "Well, is it true?"

As ever, program preparations and publicity for the next month need to take place now. PR for November's programs are October's concerns. Depending on how involved you want to get, you may actually need to be working on one of the November programs, a teen mystery night, all during October—or even begin planning it as early as September.

Figure 10.3
Urban Legends flyer

URBAN LEGENDS

FACT OR FOLKLORE?

Are there crocodiles in the sewer?
Exploding whales in Oregon?
Spider eggs in your old hairdo?

YOU decide!
(Your Date and Time)
At
(Your Library)
(Address)
(Phone Number)

Reasonable accommodation for individuals with disabilities is available.
Please contact the library prior to the event if you require accommodation.

11

❖ ❖ ❖

NOVEMBER

After the hurly-burly of Teen Read Week in October, you're probably looking forward to a quiet November. Depending on the program you choose, this month can be as easygoing or as exciting as you want. The main program, Murder in the Library, a live-action mystery event, can be set as a kind of dramatic scavenger hunt or as a full-fledged mystery party. The latter is significantly more fun. Two other options, a humanities program and a Finding Money for College program, are less labor intensive but require recruiting outside talent.

As mentioned previously, most of the programs described in this book require only about four weeks' lead time to implement. However, putting on a good program for teens is always the better for a bit more lead time and preparation. If nothing else, it's considerably less stressful. This month's main program, a library mystery game, *can* be done with a short lead time. To do it well, however, I'd recommend one of the companies that sells mystery program kits. These kits contain everything you need to run a mystery game for twenty to thirty teenagers in grades 6–9. There is no need for advance preparation in order to play the game. Otherwise, this is a program that at a minimum you'd want to begin laying the groundwork for in September.

> A terrific source for mystery program resources is DoubleDog Press at *http://www.dbldog.com/default.htm*. In addition to ready-to-go Mystery Program Kits for both kids and teens, you'll find a helpful list of author and publisher Janet Dickey's Mystery Planning tips and links to other useful sites. I wish I'd had these to refer to when I planned my first Murder in the Library program.

MYSTERY NIGHT

If you'd like to keep things simple this month, consider taking it slowly and laying the groundwork now for an all-out Mystery Night next November or as one of next year's summer programs for teens. Although I've included a complete script (a variation on several Murder in the Library scripts and programs I've done over the years) and you can run such a program all by yourself with it, why not get your local drama teacher involved? Unless you bring your own dramatic expertise to the project, you'll find her an enormous asset. Whether you want to run the program this month or next November, write your local drama teacher (or teachers) a letter briefly describing the program and asking for their expert advice. Follow up your letter with a phone call, and set up a meeting.

When you meet with the drama teacher, bring an extra copy of the script (you'll find it, a list of props, and other basic instructions at the end of this chapter), a timeline (see following pages), and a blank parental permission letter (see Chapter 3, Figure 3.2). Whether you're simply laying the groundwork for next year's mystery program or getting the current one off to a running start, ask the drama teacher how much she's willing to be involved. Would she, for example, be willing to spend time rehearsing the teens (and their understudies) on their roles? If she can do this, in addition to being your link to teens who would want to perform, you're in business. In one instance that I recall, the local high school drama teacher even gave teens who volunteered for our library program extra credit. Be sure to point out that this event can be taken "on the road" and performed in the school library as a special encore performance, either as an after-school event or (after making arrangements with the school principal and faculty) as a special in-school treat earned by deserving students.

One of the reasons for laying the groundwork early in the semester (in September) or planning this program for next summer or fall is that your local high school drama teachers may already have their curricula tightly planned. Squeezing in another project—your library's teen mystery night—may be out of the question at what seems like the last minute. If, on the other hand, the teachers can work it into their plans at the beginning of the term, it may be more appealing to them.

A timeline for the event looks something like this:

- *6 weeks prior*: Adapt the script to your local library. Begin recruiting the cast and asking local businesses or community groups to assist with prizes (optional) and/or refreshments.
- *4 weeks prior*: Your cast assembled, PR goes out to newspapers, schools, and community centers.
- *3 weeks prior*: All publicity should be complete. Have the first run-through with the cast, identifying any weak points that need work. Begin gathering props.
- *2 weeks prior*: Second rehearsal. Continue to gather props.
- *1 week prior*: All props have been made or acquired. Make calls to cast and crew to remind them of the dress rehearsal and performance dates. Make similar reminder calls to businesses or community members who have volunteered to bring treats.
- *2–4 days prior*: Dress rehearsal.
- *Performance date*.

Using the names your local drama teacher has given to you or the lists of teen volunteers you've compiled throughout the year, make recruitment phone calls. Ask these teens to participate in a live-action mystery night at the library. Use good judgment in considering whom to ask. Even though the mystery program doesn't require the kind of memorization or acting skills of, say, *Bye-Bye Birdie* or *The Crucible*, this is not the kind of event at which the painfully shy or inarticulate will shine. You don't want to set these young people up for failure. Ideally, there should be two volunteers for each of the four roles (that of the murder victim is played, as it were, in absentia): a main cast member and an understudy.

Obviously, the big commitment is to the actual performance date, but be sure that the young people you approach are aware of the time commitment to rehearse as well. It's also useful to ask them to give you a rough idea of their schedules—"such and such hours for school," "these dates and times for the volleyball team, band practice, etc." Staple a master cast list to your own master copy of the script, and keep it handy whenever you're working on the program.

I learned of the importance of this arrangement, including the need to have understudies, the hard way. Less than a week before we were due for our first show (it was repeated at two other libraries), two of our main cast members dropped out! We found one new cast member, rewrote one part so that it could be played in absentia, and squeezed in an extra rehearsal. In the event that you're pinched for teen volunteers, two of the roles (the reference librarian and the library clerk) can easily be played by staff members while working at the reference or circulation desk.

Once you have a cast, you'll want to decide on a location and a time. Are you going to hold the event during normal library hours? If so, will you attempt to have it take place entirely within the meeting room or similar space? I have held Mystery Nights that are effective either way. If, however, you choose to do anything other than hold the event during normal library hours entirely in the meeting room, you'll need to meet with your director to plan the event. After-hours programs involve compensation for library staff and similar issues. Events held during normal hours but moving throughout the library require your director to balance the needs of the general community, stress to the other staff, and the exigencies of your program.

Although solving the mystery is its own reward and the fun is in the doing, you can, if you choose, give a prize to the winner, that is, the participant who figures out who committed the crime. If there is more than one winner, hold an impromptu drawing. Any left-over (or held back) summer reading program prizes will work well; but if you plan

---

Of course, you always write thank-you letters to volunteers and to local businesspeople who provide money, prizes, or other assistance for library programs. But you should also consider providing some public acknowledgment of the generosity of your sponsors. For local business owners and community service agencies, being seen as a generous and helpful member of the community is very important.

Whenever it's appropriate, in your flyers or in small 8½" × 14" (legal size) posters in the library on the day of event, say "thank you" to your sponsors. It need not be flowery or effusive. "This program was made possible by the generous assistance of [Name of business, community group, or agency]" works quite well.

Whenever you present a large program that requires volunteer assistance and involvement from a variety of sources (as the Mystery Night one can), you should also consider writing a letter of praise to the local paper. It's another way to publicly acknowledge people and motivate them to say "yes" to your future requests.

to make a major production of the event, you should contact local businesses, community service groups, or the Friends of the Library group and ask for a special donation. You'll certainly want to round up help in providing drinks and snacks. In addition to asking fellow staff members to help out, contact local restaurants, pizza parlors, supermarkets, and delis and request donations.

With prizes, refreshments, cast, and location lined up, you'll need to set up a rehearsal schedule. If you're quite lucky, the local high school drama teacher is handling this for you. If, as is more often the case, the job devolves on you, don't despair. As difficult as it may seem to get four to eight busy teens together on the same day, it isn't really a difficulty you have to face. The mystery script is designed to allow cast members to practice somewhat independently of one another. There are no scenes and no by-play (although if you're working with a bunch of rampant extroverts, they'll probably come up with their own).

Set up three rehearsals to which the majority of the cast can come at least once. Only the final performance date is mandatory. At each rehearsal, go over the basic outline of events: the introduction to the crime scene and physical evidence, the interviewing of the suspects (your cast), the voting by the participants, and the conclusion in which the solution is revealed. Have cast members take turns pretending to be participants and asking questions based on the Crime Reports (Figure 11.1) that the actual participants will be using. Make a list of any costume items or props that the cast can bring, and write them down on your master cast list as you tick them off the checklist provided with the script. A detailed checklist of props, as well as a more detailed description of the program night, is contained in the Murder in the Library: A Solve-It-Yourself Mystery script at the end of this chapter.

To publicize the program, set up a display of teen mystery novels with a border of crime scene tape next to your flyer. Or tack up the same border on a bulletin board display with a booklist of teen mystery novels

---

For some first-rate teen mystery novels to add to those from the adult mystery collection, look for the Edgar Award sponsored by the Mystery Writers of America, Inc. (*http://www.mysterywriters.net/*). This group's Young Adult award goes out to truly exciting, well-written examples of the genre with terrific YA appeal. Even if you aren't personally interested in the genre, these are sure-fire hits. You can find a "back list" of Edgar (and other award) winners in *Literary Laurels: A Reader's Guide to Award-Winning Fiction*, edited by Laura Carlson, Sean Creighton, and Sheila Cunningham (Hillyard, 1995).

Figure 11.1
Mystery Night crime report

Crime Report

Some things to think about when you question the suspects:
Where was the suspect today?
Did they have a motive to kill B. G. Bossman?
Did they have the means or the opportunity to kill B. G. Bossman?
Does the suspect have an alibi?
Don't forget to examine the physical evidence (Exhibits A - E) and the crime scene!

HELPFUL	MORGAN
ASKME	PAT C.

You've asked your questions, taken notes and now you're ready to name the villain!

Your name: _____

Who committed the crime, how and why? _____

_____

_____

(Continue on the back if you need to)

in a pocket holder (see Chapter 1, Figure 1.3). A sample program flyer is shown in Figure 11.2. Send copies to every business that volunteered either prizes or refreshments and to community centers and schools. Write to your local papers about the event. See Figure 11.3 for a sample letter.

Follow up the successful completion of your program with thank-you letters and, if your budget (or your Friends of the Library group's budget) permits, with a cast party for the teens. I've often paid to have pizza delivered shortly after we cleaned up and put things away. It was a chance not only to celebrate and give tangible form to my appreciation of their hard work and creativity, but to debrief them about what went right, what went wrong, and whether they'd want to do it again.

HUMANITIES PROGRAMS

An alternate event for mid-fall that usually proves attractive to local high school English, drama, or social studies faculty involves state and local humanities programming. Does your state have (as does Washington's) a Commission for the Humanities (*http://www.humanities.org/*)? These organizations offer excellent programs for adults, some of which are of interest to teens as well. Recognizing that public libraries are among the important community cultural institutions, your state humanities commission may be willing to offer you a steep discount. A program that would cost $400 might be offered to you through your Friends of the Library group at $75.

Do local community colleges have guest speakers or lecturers whom you could invite to the library for a local fee? Are there local drama groups (such as the Seattle Children's Theatre) who'd be willing to perform excerpts from, say, Shakespeare for a teen and adult audience at your library? Your library has a good name in the community and in many minds is intimately linked with the notion of great literature and high culture. Why not take advantage of this to invite speakers or performers for your teen audience?

In addition, once booked, these programs have natural PR appeal. Write a letter to your local paper informing the public of the event. On a slow news day the local paper might send a photographer and write up the event. Write to the local schools, emphasizing the educational and cultural value of the event. Teachers may even offer extra credit to their students for attending.

Figure 11.2
Mystery Night flyer

Who did the deed?
Who knows the secret?
YOU solve the crime
(Your date)
(Your Time)

Join us for a night of mystery, clues, and
tasty refreshments at
(Your Library).

The Mystery Night at the Library is made possible
by a generous donation from
(Your sponsors).

(Your Address • Phone number)

Reasonable accommodation for individuals with disabilities is available.
Please contact the library prior to the event if you require accommodation.

Figure 11.3
Letter to local papers

[Name of Local Paper's Community Events editor—call to find out]
[Name of Local Newspaper]
[Address]
[Fax and Phone Numbers]

Dear [Events Editor],

This month, on [date and time of your program], the [Name of your library] and teens from [Names of the schools from which your teen cast comes] will be hosting Murder at the Library, a live-action mystery game for our community. It's sure to be an exciting program, and our young people have worked hard to bring this event to life. [If you have the involvement of your local high school drama teacher, add here, "especially because (Name of drama teacher) has brought her expertise to casting and directing the drama."]

I hope you will feature this event in your [Name of the Community Events section] of [Name of local newspaper]. If you have any questions or concerns, please don't hesitate to contact me at [Name of your library] at [your library's address, phone number, and, if applicable, your e-mail address]. I'm generally available at [your shift dates and times].

Another program to consider that requires a local expert is Finding Money for College. Every fall, at different branches, the King County Library System hosts a seminar for the parents and guardians of college-bound teens. We work with CPN, the College Planning Network (*http://www.collegeplan.org/*), to provide a seminar for parents of college-bound teens about scholarships and other financial aid for their children.

Why not set up a similar arrangement at your library? Your resources include not only nonprofit programs such as Dollars for Scholars, a key program of the nonprofit Citizen's Scholarship Foundations of America (*http://www.csfa.org/*), but also the financial aid departments of local colleges and universities. Invite the financial aid officer of the nearest college to speak to parents and teens. Have available copies of the Free Application for Federal Student Aid (FAFSA) from the U.S. Department of Education at *http://www.ed.gov/offices/OPE/express.html* and of the CSS/Financial Aid Profile from The College Board at *http://www.collegeboard.org/finaid/fas-taff/profile/html/indx000.html*.

However busy you plan to make your November, relax a bit by preparing for a simple (but fun) craft program next month. As ever, you'll need to begin your publicity and preparations this month for next month's events.

APPENDIX: MURDER IN THE LIBRARY, A SOLVE-IT-YOURSELF MYSTERY SCRIPT

Cast of Characters

B. G. Bossman, the nasty library director (and presumed murder victim)

T. Ryanne (or Ryan) Askme, the wimpy reference librarian

Morgan Doobeygoode Gaylord, the wealthy library patron

I. B. Helpful, the teen library volunteer

Pat C. Bossman, the director's sister and library clerk

Timetable

Pat C. and Helpful arrive at the library	4 hours	(1:00 P.M.)
Askme arrives late	3¾ hours	(1:15 P.M.)
Bossman arrives at the library	3½ hours	(1:30 P.M.)
Askme accosts Bossman		
Morgan arrives for meeting with Bossman	45 minutes	(4:15 P.M.)
Morgan storms out and meets with Askme	40 minutes	(4:20 P.M.)
Helpful sneaks into Bossman's office	30 minutes	(4:30 P.M.)
Bossman fakes her own death	15 minutes	(4:45 P.M.)
Bossman's "murder" is discovered	0 hour	(5:00 P.M.)

[*Notes*: Depending on your setting, Bossman can be in hiding in the library, waiting to escape later, or have already fled through a door or window in her office.]

Cast and Clues

[*Note*: Although I refer to all cast members as "she," these roles can be played by males or females.]

Victim/Murderer: Library Director, B. G. (Bob or Birgit Gomer) Bossman

Costume/Appearance: N/A
Station: A pile of ashes at the crime scene

Character: Not really applicable, but bossy, manipulative, and unscrupulous

Motive: Bossman ran off with the overdue fines collection to finance a new life in Barbados. Bossman had to go because Askme (the reference librarian) was about to break down, confess her (or his) earlier embezzlement, and press charges against Bossman for blackmailing.

Opportunity: Bossman unlocked the safe containing the fine money (which was collected in the safe each day until weekend delivery to the bank) and stole it. Bossman "died" approximately 15 minutes before her "death" was discovered. This should be at the start time of your program. So, for example (as shown in the timetable), if your program begins at 5 P.M., Bossman's disappearance or "death" would have taken place at 4:45 P.M. Bossman hid in a closet (or a storeroom or under a desk) when Helpful was searching for evidence. After Bossman faked her death, depending on your library's setting, Bossman can either remain in hiding or have escaped through an unguarded door or window.

Alibi: Bossman appears to be dead by spontaneous human combustion.

Proof: There are three ways to prove the case. *By elimination*: Each suspect's alibis back up the others'. No one could have done it. *From clues*: There's a book at the crime scene, *How to Disappear Completely and Never Be Found*. (There are real books with titles like this, or you could create your own dummy title and book cover.) *From the testimony of the other suspects*: Morgan sold Bossman a flamethrower gun; the reference librarian had already confessed to both Helpful and Pat C., who'd convinced Askme to confess and go to the police. Askme also recalls Bossman asking her to do a reference search on strange and weird ways to die. Pat C. recalls checking out a stack of books on Barbados and spontaneous human combustion. Pat C. can confirm that B. G. Bossman had the only keys to the safe. Helpful recalls seeing Bossman reading books on Barbados and helped her log on to a "buy your plane tickets anonymously on-line" website. She also recalls having to wait for a refund on a CD that helpful lost, then found again until Bossman was available with keys to the safe.

Reference Librarian: T. Ryanne (or Ryan) Askme

Costume/Appearance: Ordinary, conservative clothes; no shoes

Station: Standing right by the reference desk

Character: Nervous, fussy, and slightly prissy. The stereotypical reference librarian with hair in a bun and a finger half-raised to "shush." Askme, however, has a sympathetic and friendly nature and would be willing to take a risk to help someone in need.

Motive: Askme borrowed library fines to pay for a kidney for her sick mother. She repaid the money, but B. G. Bossman found out and blackmailed Askme. Now the fine money has gone missing again.

Opportunity: Askme called in sick but secretly met with Bossman outside the library that morning. She never went home but hung around trying to talk with Bossman again. Askme could have snuck in the "back way" (using the same method Bossman did to sneak out). An empty can of gasoline was found in her car. She has matches in her pocket.

Alibi: Askme never actually went into the library building again after meeting secretly with Bossman. Pat C. worked all day and never saw Askme enter the building. The grounds outside the library were muddy, and if she'd come back in she would have left muddy footprints inside. No such prints were found. After meeting with Bossman, but before Morgan arrived, Helpful came outside to find out why Askme was skulking around the library. Askme broke down and confessed, telling Helpful about stealing the fine money to pay for her mother's emergency kidney operation, paying it back, and being blackmailed by Bossman. Although Helpful was a bit disgusted by Askme's waffling, Helpful said that Askme should follow through on her threat to Bossman to expose the blackmail. After her loud and argumentative meeting with Bossman, Morgan stormed outside and can confirm that Morgan ran into Askme and spent the rest of the day commiserating on how awful Bossman was. Morgan was with Askme the entire time until the Inspector called them in as suspects.

Clues: [Cast members are encouraged to learn these by heart but in a pinch can carry a prop, such as a notebook, in which they can place the clues and refer to them as needed. More important is to behave "in character" and respond to questions as if one really were T. Ryanne Askme.]

- Askme says that she (or he) was simply refilling her gasoline can in order to get more gas for her lawnmower.
- Askme's boyfriend (or girlfriend) is a smoker, which is why Askme has matches.
- Askme already confessed her crime last week to both Helpful and to Pat. C., who have encouraged her to come clean about the offense and to go after Bossman.
- Askme will admit she dislikes and fears Bossman and, when she accosted Bossman before Bossman went into the library that day, threatened tell the police about Bossman's blackmail. Askme will

add that Bossman seemed not to care, telling Askme that Bossman would see to it that Askme went to prison, too.

• Askme can tell about Bossman's reference request for unusual ways to die.

• Askme used to have the only other set of keys to the library safe, but she hasn't had them since she stole the fines to pay for her sick mother's operation.

• Regarding Morgan, Askme can describe how Bossman tricked Morgan into buying the library carts for the library just before the last mayoral election and how silly Morgan looked. Askme voted against Morgan in the mayoral election, "like most people I know." Askme is aware of a big fight Morgan had with Bossman that afternoon because Morgan stormed out of the library afterwards. "Everybody heard the fight." Askme will confirm that Morgan was with her from about 40 minutes prior to discovery of the "body" (i.e., the program start time).

• Askme is in stocking feet. If asked why, Askme admits that her shoes were so wet and mud-soaked that she was asked to take them off and leave them outside.

• Regarding Helpful, Askme can tell how surprised and upset Askme felt when Helpful didn't get the new library clerk/page job because Helpful is such a great volunteer. Askme knows how important Helpful's other volunteer work at PFAB-WWGEF-SPAS (People for a Better World Without Guns Except for Some Police and Soldiers) is to Helpful and how committed Helpful is to the cause of nonviolence. Askme is sorry that Helpful's Ska band's contract to play for the library was cancelled by Bossman, especially because Askme helped set up the concert in the first place.

• If asked about Pat C. Bossman, Askme will tell how the other Bossman (his or her sister Pat C.) turned out to be much nicer than B. G. Bossman but is totally inept as a library clerk/page. Askme can't imagine how someone like Pat C. ever got hired. Askme could see Pat C. through one or more of the library windows while Askme was dithering outside the library, trying to get up enough courage to call the police and confront Bossman. Askme will confirm that Pat C. never leaves the checkout desk. Askme thinks that Pat C. is a truly terrible library clerk—"That nice I. B. Helpful would have done such a better job!"—but feels very sorry for her. Askme knows the story of how Bossman keeps her sister (or brother) cowed, how Bossman cheated Pat C. of her inheritance when their parents died and forced Pat C. to act as an unpaid housekeeper, and how Pat C. needs the minimum wage library job to save up enough money to "escape" Bossman.

- If asked whether Askme heard or saw anything unusual, Askme will admit to having heard a strange muffled roar coming from what Askme thinks is the direction of Bossman's office at 4:45 P.M. (that is, 15 minutes before your program is scheduled to start) but does not know what the roar was except that Askme has heard similar sounds lately when Helpful's band was rehearsing last week.

Wealthy Library Patron: Morgan Doobeygoode Gaylord (Or "Brodart" or whichever company your library purchased its book carts from)

Costume/Appearance: Stylish or rich-looking clothes (if a female character, lots of costume jewelry). Several mock-up business cards with Morgan's name and his or her company's name and motto: "Doobeygoode Compact Flamethrowers—No job too small, no gun too big!"

Station: Anywhere

Character: Morgan is a loud, extroverted person with a hot temper but a genuinely good heart.

Motive: Bossman convinced Doobeygoode to donate money for new library carts by telling Morgan that Morgan's name would appear on every cart. Bossman then purchased the carts from a supply company with same last name as Morgan. Morgan is now a laughingstock and lost the mayoral election as a result.

Opportunity: Morgan was the last person to see Bossman alive. Morgan also owns the country's largest flamethrower gun–manufacturing plant.

Alibi: She secretly sold several more flamethrowers to the Ska band Non-Abrasive Wet System for their next concert. Morgan doesn't know why this meeting has to be kept secret, but Morgan's buyer, I. B. Helpful, insists that the sale is off if anyone finds out about it. Askme will confirm that Morgan was with her from the time Morgan stormed out of Bossman's office to the time the "body" was discovered and the Inspector brought them in as suspects.

Clues: A prop for the teen playing Morgan in which to hide a "cheat sheet" for the clues could be a day-planner or similar notebook.

- Morgan sold Bossman a flamethrower gun. Bossman told Morgan it was a "peace offering" after the debacle with the library carts. Bossman said she had a big buyer who would contract for hundreds of the guns if the buyer could check out a sample. Morgan was afraid it was another scam and that she'd just look foolish again, so she kept it very quiet.

- Morgan met with Bossman about 45 minutes before the program start time (4:15 P.M. if you assume a 5 P.M. start time). Morgan will admit that they fought. Morgan set up the meeting to see if Bossman's "big buyer" was real but lost her temper and began yelling, calling Bossman a liar, a cheat, and a thief. Bossman yelled back, calling Morgan names Morgan won't repeat. "They were too awful!" Bossman threatened to call the police and have Morgan thrown out. "It kind of got out of hand." Morgan will admit that she's still very upset about the incident with the carts and angry about losing the election. Morgan blames Bossman and says that if anyone deserved to get flamed, it was Bossman.

- Regarding Askme, Morgan left the building and immediately ran into the reference librarian. In Morgan's opinion, Askme is a wimp but a good librarian. Morgan spent the next 40 minutes, before the Inspector arrived and called them in as suspects, talking to Askme about what a rat her boss was. Morgan will confirm that Askme's shoes were wet and muddy.

- Regarding Helpful, Morgan thought she was just "another punk kid" but when Helpful brought a Doobeygoode flamethrower gun to a meeting with Morgan and offered to purchase more, Morgan changed her mind. "Treat the customer right, make the sale, I always say." Morgan is also surprised that Helpful wants the sale to be kept completely secret, but she doesn't mind. "The customer is always right."

- Regarding Pat C., Morgan says she thought she would dislike Pat C. because she's related to Bossman, but now Morgan says that Pat C. is a pain no matter who she's related to. Morgan thinks Pat C. is utterly inept. Morgan finds this very irritating. "She never leaves the checkout desk, she just looks stupid and points. It's as if her rear end was glued to the stupid chair!"

- Morgan saw Pat C. at the checkout desk when Morgan arrived for her meeting with Bossman and also when she stormed out of the library.

Teen Volunteer: I. B. Helpful (Member of the Ska band Non-Abrasive Wet System)

Costume/Appearance: Ordinary teen. Has a "contract" for several Doobeygoode Compact Flamethrowers purchased for his or her band, "Non-Abrasive Wet System" (Exhibit E in "Evidence & Props" list).

Station: By a book cart

Character: A nice if somewhat pushy person. Tends to be a bit unrealistic about life but is very passionate about nonviolence and her band.

Motive: Volunteered for Bossman under the impression that she (or he) would have first shot at a newly created library clerk/page job. Bossman not only gave the job to Bossman's sister (or brother), Pat C., but Bossman cancelled Non-Abrasive Wet System's contract to perform a concert for the library's Teen Summer Reading program kick-off event. One of the band members brought his dad's Doobeygoode Gargantuan Flamethrower to the Ska band's last rehearsal, and the band members all thought they could use flamethrowers to make cool special effects for their next concert. Helpful hung onto the flamethrower gun to show to Morgan when negotiating for more of them for Helpful's band.

Opportunity: Helpful secretly snuck into Bossman's office looking for proof that Bossman had cheated with regard to the job posting. She thought she may have found it when she heard a noise; Helpful dropped the file folder and fled.

Alibi: Helpful had a secret meeting with Morgan to purchase flamethrowing guns to use for special effects in Non-Abrasive Wet System's next concert. Helpful was afraid if word got out that she was buying a large gun, she would be kicked out of PFAB-WWGEF-SPAS (People for a Better World Without Guns Except for Some Police and Soldiers). Helpful is a serious pacifist and would never consider violence. Pat C. will confirm that she saw Helpful step into Bossman's office and that Helpful was not carrying anything or hiding any large objects such as a flamethrowing gun.

Clues: A good "cheat sheet" prop for Helpful would be a library book on music or nonviolence.

- Regarding Bossman, Helpful recalls showing Bossman how to log on to the Internet and find a site that lets you purchase airplane tickets anonymously on-line. Helpful will admit that the library concert was going to be her band's big break. "They were going to pay us and everything!" She's really angry with Bossman for canceling it. Helpful thinks that if she could prove "the truth" about Pat C., she could pressure Bossman into reinstating the concert.

- Helpful is a member of PFAB-WWGEF-SPAS because she really, really doesn't like violence or killing. PFAB-WWGEF-SPAS is the most important thing in her life except for her band.

- Regarding Morgan, Helpful wants her band to succeed and thinks that Doobeygoode Flamethrower Guns are just the thing to make cool special effects. Morgan is "pretty cool for a suit" and helpful about getting the guns secretly. Morgan says she'd never use the flamethrower guns as *guns*; "It would be against my principles."

- Regarding Pat C., Helpful used to be mad at her for getting the job that Bossman had promised to Helpful if Helpful would volunteer 20 hours a week at the library for six months. But now Helpful thinks of Pat C. as "another one of Bossman's victims." Helpful still wants the library clerk job because Pat C. isn't very good at it, and sometimes Pat C. makes people mad because Pat C. won't leave the checkout/reference desk. "She just sits there and points. That flamethrower gal (or guy) Morgan really got mad at Pat C. for that."

- Helpful will admit to snooping in Bossman's office. Helpful wanted to talk to Bossman about the concert, but when she opened the door Bossman was nowhere to be seen (Bossman was hiding under the desk). Snooping through Bossman's files, Helpful found the job applications both she and Pat C. had turned in; but before Helpful could really look at them, Helpful heard a noise, got nervous, and fled.

Library Clerk/Page: Pat C. Bossman (Pronounced "Patsy"; Bossman's brother—or sister)

Costume/Appearance: Disheveled

Station: By the circulation desk

Character: A weak, easily victimized person. Pat C. is totally in her (or his) sister's (or brother's) shadow and frightened of Bossman. Pat C. doesn't want to admit that her sister is a rat, and she makes excuses for Bossman. Pat C. is unwilling to believe or say bad things about anyone.

Motive: Pat C. has an excellent motive. Constantly in Bossman's shadow, Pat C. never went to college or got a job but lived with her parents. When they died unexpectedly, Bossman cheated Pat C. out of her inheritance and threatened to throw her out into the street unless she became Bossman's unpaid housekeeper, cook, and flunky. Bossman got Pat C. the job of library clerk/page because it would keep her under Bossman's thumb.

Opportunity: Pat C. has had no opportunity to harm Bossman. Because Bossman appears to have been murdered by being set on fire or by someone with a flamethrower, it is impossible for Pat C. to have committed the crime. Pat C., however, not wishing to believe any of the nice people at the library could do anything so nasty as commit murder, is convinced that Bossman died of spontaneous human combustion.

Alibi: Pat C. was at the checkout/reference desk all day. Helpful, Askme, and Morgan will all confirm that Pat C. doesn't leave the desk. Pat C. will admit that this is true, as she does not feel that she can do a good job helping people. Because she desperately needs the job, any job, if she is to have enough money to "escape" Bossman, Pat C. attempts to hide her inability by staying put and doing the bare minimum. "If I just stay behind the desk and point, they'll give up and go to Askme."

Clues: A "cheat sheet" prompt for Pat C. could be a library manual.

- Pat C. will readily admit she's frightened of Bossman and won't leave the checkout/reference desk, not even to take a break, unless Bossman tells her to.

- Pat C. checked out a stack of books to Bossman that were all about Barbados and about spontaneous human combustion. Pat C. thinks that perhaps Bossman, her "poor sister (or brother)," had a premonition about dying by spontaneous combustion.

- Regarding Askme, Pat C. feels terribly sorry for her. Just the other day, Askme broke down and told Pat C. how she "borrowed" the fine money from the safe to pay for her mother's new kidney, and how Bossman found out and was blackmailing Askme. Pat C. advised Askme to come clean to the police and confront Bossman. Pat C. says that although Askme called in sick today, Pat C. could see Askme through the windows hanging around outside. Pat C. did not see Askme try to talk to Bossman before Bossman went into the library. Pat C. can confirm that she never saw Askme come into the library.

- Pat C. was the person who told Askme to take her shoes off because they would track mud into the library.

- Regarding Morgan, Pat C. only knows that "she's got a bit of a temper" and that Bossman made a public fool of Morgan over the library cart donation. Pat C. didn't vote for Morgan either. Pat C. saw Morgan come in about 45 minutes prior to the discovery of Bossman's "body" (your program's start time) and leave after 5 minutes. The fight between Bossman and Morgan was loud and noisy.

- Regarding Helpful, Pat C. admits that Helpful does most of the work. "All I really know how to do is check books in and out and take fines." Pat C. recalls how irritated I. B. Helpful got when Pat C. couldn't give Helpful a refund on a CD Helpful had lost, paid for, then found again because there wasn't enough money in the cash register (or money drawer). When Pat C. pointed to Askme, Askme admitted to both Helpful and Pat C. that she no longer had the keys. Only Bossman had the keys to the safe.

- Pat C. saw Helpful go into Bossman's office, but Helpful wasn't carrying or hiding anything, certainly not a flamethrower.

- Pat C. heard a muffled roaring sound coming from Bossman's office about 15 minutes prior to the discovery of the body. It was the same kind of sound she had heard a few times when Helpful's band, Non-Abrasive Wet System, was practicing in the library meeting room. Pat C. was still at the checkout/reference desk when the Inspector brought Pat C. in as a suspect.

The Inspector (Librarian or volunteer staff running the program)

Costume/Appearance: Trench coat and hat

Dramatic Conclusion

Although the character B. G. Bossman can be played, as it were, in absentia, capping off the program with a dramatic confrontation can be fun. If Bossman is hiding out in the library, waiting for a chance to sneak off to Barbados, she can be dragged out by an angry cast member (Helpful or even Askme) and confronted. If Bossman fled through a window or back door, she can be dragged back by the Inspector, whose agents caught her at the airport. Either way, this is appropriate when you have an enthusiastic group of young actors who'd like a chance to script a confrontation and ham it up.

Evidence & Props

• pile of ashes (at the crime scene)

• file folder labeled "Library Clerk" (Exhibit A)

• one of your library clerk (or page) applications with no information filled in except Pat C. Bossman's name

• another such application completely and glowingly filled in for I. B. Helpful. Previous experience listed includes volunteering at the Humane Society, serving as junior vice president for the political committee People for a Better World Without Guns, Except for Some Police and Soldiers (PFAB-WWGEF-SPAS), and volunteering for the library. Interests/activities should be filled in with "drummer for the Non-Abrasive Wet System Ska band," and References should be filled in with the name T. Ryan Askme. (Inside the "Library Clerk" folder)

• an empty can labeled "gasoline" (Exhibit B)

• a matchbook with most of the matches torn out (Exhibit C)

• a stack (as many as you expect to have teen participants) of homemade business cards with Morgan's name (his or her last name depends on the brand of library cart your library uses; our carts came from Gaylord, so Morgan's full name becomes Morgan Doobeygoode Gaylord); Morgan's company name, Doobeygoode

Figure 11.4
Mystery Night Doobeygoode's props

DOOBEYGOODE FLAMEFLOWERS
111 GELIGNITE LANE
SPRINGFIELD, NA 12345
WWW.SETFIRETOIT.COM

"NO JOB TOO SMALL, NO GUN TOO BIG!"

Morgan Doobeygoode Gaylord, President
(123) 456-7890

DOOBEYGOODE FLAMETHROWERS
111 Geligntite Lane
Springfield, NA 12345
www.setitonfire.com

ORDER FORM

Order via the internet: www.setitonfire.com
Or call: 123-456-7890

Office Hours: Monday - Saturday 1 - 8 pm NST
Orders are invoiced at time of order.
The minimum shipping charge is $5.00.
Shipping may not be legal in most states.

Bill To:	Ship To:
Name: *I. B. Helpful*	Name: *Non-Abrasive Wet System*
Account No: *XXX-YYY-ZZZ*	Account No: *XXX-YYY-ZZZ*
Address: *123 Big Band Blvd #BB*	Address: *123 Big Band Blvd #BB*
Springfield, NA 12345	*Springfield NA, 12345*
Phone: 123-111-2222 Fax: *Don't have one*	Phone: 123-111-2222 Fax: *Don't have one*

Item No.	Size	Description	Quantity	Unit Price	Total
A-123	*Huge*	*Giant Size Flamethrower Gun*	*5*	$45.00	$225.00
				Sales Tax:	$25.00
					$250.00

THANK YOU FOR YOUR ORDER!

Compact Flamethrowers, and motto, "No job too small, no gun too big!"; plus a fake phone number such as 555–123–4567 (Figure 11.4).

• a fake "contract" for several Doobeygoode Compact Flamethrowers sold to Non-Abrasive Wet System and signed by I. B. Helpful (Figure 11.4).

• trench coat for the Inspector

• badge for the Inspector

• nametags or badges for the suspects

• evidence table

• library director's desk and chair

• a mock-up nameplate for "B. G. Bossman, Library Director"

• a dummy safe, empty, with the door open; or a drawing or photocopy of a safe in the same condition tacked to the wall beside Bossman's desk

• tags reading "Exhibit A," "Exhibit B," "Exhibit C," "Exhibit D," and "Exhibit E"

• police crime scene tape (available at novelty shops, but you might be able to get local police to donate a roll)

• crime reports (on the Evidence Table) used to write down notes; these also contain sample questions to get the participants started, as well as a spot to "vote" on the solution to the crime (Figure 11.1)

• pencils (as many as you expect teen participants)

• police report (on the Evidence Table)

• box labeled "Solutions"

Set

• a crime scene: If you have a cooperative library director, this will be her office, marked off with police tape. Otherwise, you'll need to set up a desk and chair in a corner of the meeting room with the dummy nameplate prominently displayed, the dummy safe or mock-up, and the entire "scene" marked off with the police tape.

• a table off to one side labeled "Evidence" and displaying Exhibits A–E, a box labeled "Solutions," and a stack of crime reports and sharpened pencils

• a refreshments table

• food, drink, napkins, cups, and plates

Scenario

Prepare the crime scene, evidence, and refreshment tables. Make sure the cast is in costume and in place. Once teen participants have arrived and had a chance to nibble and chat in a meeting room (or a separate area with drinks and snacks), the Inspector asks for the attention of the group and announces the following:

"Ladies and gentlemen, I regret to inform you that a serious crime has been discovered. Robbery and *murder*. I have preserved the crime scene, the evidence, the preliminary police report, and all the suspects."

"Your mission, should you choose to accept it, is to view the crime scene, examine the evidence, and question the suspects. When you believe that you have successfully solved the crime, write down your solution to the mystery on a Crime Report sheet. Place the report in that box [point to the box labeled "Solutions" near the refreshments table]. When everyone has come up with a solution, we'll examine the reports and learn the truth."

"Please pick up your Crime Reports at the evidence table, and begin!"

At this point the Inspector takes the teens out to view the crime scene and the evidence table (encouraging the participants to look at but not to touch the former, and to handle but not to remove the latter). Depending on whether this program plays out in the main library or entirely in the meeting room, the suspects (wearing nametags labeled "Suspect: I. B. Helpful" and the like) will be located at their stations, to which the Inspector will shepherd participants and point out each suspect. Alternately, the Inspector will hustle the suspects into the meeting room and introduce them. Either way, at this point the Inspector acts as a moderator, encouraging questions.

Once everyone thinks they have a solution, or about 20 minutes before the program is due to end, the Inspector rounds up the participants and herds them back toward the refreshments area for the conclusion. Taking out the entries, the Inspector reads aloud every *wrong* solution (setting aside correct or mostly correct answers until the last) in turn, explaining why it can't work based on the available clues. Similar wrong answers can be skipped. When the last wrong answer has been read, the Inspector turns to the correct answers, reads them aloud without comment, and concludes:

"That's right, ladies and gentlemen. That no-good louse, B. G. Bossman, embezzled the fine money, framed the reference librarian, faked her own death, and fled to Barbados! The murderer is—the victim!"

12

DECEMBER

As the country becomes increasingly diverse, it is important that librarians (as public officials) take into account the variety of "end of the year" and winter celebrations among the many cultures—Jewish, Christian, Wiccan, Muslim, and more—that make up the communities we serve. A "holiday" program celebrating Christmas simply can no longer be the default event. Nonetheless, the turning of the year is a popular time for people of many different cultures, and traditionally for Americans, to give gifts. A gift-making program for teens can focus on the personal touch and the personal relationship, no matter what holiday they celebrate.

A variety of fun projects can be done with teens; jewelry making is always popular, as are basket making and decoration. There are any number of craft books that adults use around this time of year. The questions to ask yourself are: Can I afford the materials for the number of teens I expect to draw? Are the instructions sufficiently clear that with a minimum of practice I can learn the skill well enough to abstract the important steps and teach it? Can it be done without any special knowledge or talent in the arts, that is, can most teens succeed? Is it a product that an adult would be willing to pay good money for if it were for sale?

GLASS ORNAMENT CRAFT PROJECT

One of my favorites is a glass globe craft that is easy, inexpensive, and fun. I've used it with seashells and sand in July, and with glitter and gold at the turn of the year. You'll need:

- clear glass ornaments (minimum one per teen but you may wish to have a few extras in case of accidents)
- gold and silver craft paints and at least two other paint colors that won't be unattractive when mixed; red and green, for example, usually blend to a dull brown, but red and blue or green and blue can be quite pretty (one 2 oz. bottle of paint per teen, expecting the participants to mix and match)
- inexpensive narrow ribbons in matching shades (about 6" per teen)
- paper towels (1 sheet per teen, cut in half)
- a water source, either small paper cups with about 1" of water per teen or a nearby sink and tap
- a soft cloth—a dishtowel or pad of paper towels—one per teen, on which they can rest their ornament
- a trashcan lined with a plastic trash bag or liner

Have at least one finished ornament to show the participants what they can expect, and one extra unfinished ornament for demonstration purposes.

The actual process, although it can take a few minutes, is quite easy. Carefully pull the gold-colored top from the ornament to expose the bare rim of glass. Then, simply dribble a few lines of no more than four colors of paint inside. Dribble a few drops of water into the glass ball. Then fold a small paper towel into quarters and using it as a pad to protect your thumb, cap the top with your thumb, gently holding on to the glass (too much pressure could cause it to break) and shake vigorously. As I demonstrate it, this is a full arm movement relying on centripetal force to swirl the paint around, so be sure to give yourself plenty of room. Add more paint as needed to fully cover the inside of the glass globe. When finished, recap the glass ball, cut a piece of ribbon to act as a bow, and tie it on. For those teens who use considerably more paint than is needed, have a trashcan handy for them to drain their globe into before capping it off.

Whenever you're doing a "Hey, look what you could learn to make—

free!" program, it's a good idea to publicize it with some "show and tell." Make a few sample glass ornaments to share with local school librarians, asking them to display the sample with your flyer. A sample flyer is shown in Figure 12.1. If you attach a loop of ribbon, both the flyer and the sample ornament can be stapled or taped to a display area or bulletin board. Add Jean Thesman's charming *The Ornament Tree* (Avon Books, 1998), an Anne of Green Gables–type story set in turn-of-the-century Seattle, and appropriate craft books to your display. Your Question Board might read, "If you could afford to do anything, what would your dream holiday vacation be?"

GAME NIGHT

Another popular event to start up during the winter school holidays, if you have access to a decent-sized meeting room, is a regular game night. It does require the participation of a community expert if you want to make this a regular library feature for teens. Chess clubs are often popular: Contact your local high school to see if a club might like to use the library meeting room once a week.

For assistance in getting a regular chess night for teens and older children started in your library, visit *http://www.uschess.org/*, the website of the United States Chess Federation. This website has links to local chess clubs nationwide. The National Scholastic Chess Foundation at *http://www.nscfchess.org/nscfmiss.htm* might also prove useful.

Also popular with teens are such trading card games as Magic, The Gathering. To get one started, contact Wizards of the Coast at *http://www.wizards.com/*. It's a remarkably library-friendly company. It might be fun to connect with them while they bring out (it's still in development as I write) their new "Harry Potter" game based on the best-selling books by J. K. Rowling.

If you feel up to the challenge, why not try running a module or single scenario of a role-playing game (RPG)? *Dungeons and Dragons*, the most widely known example, is the easiest but also the least interesting sort of RPG. Your first short group storytelling experience (which is what all the best games become, mixed in with a bit of improvisational theater) could be a one-time treat introducing teens to the world of gaming. Alternatively, it could serve as a kick-off program for a regular once-a-week game night. I've run several such scenarios for teens, including one set in the imaginary (and hilarious) city of Ankh-Morpork using *GURPS DiscWorld* by Phil Masters, Terry Pratchett, and Paul Kilby. Running a

Figure 12.1
Glass Globe Craft flyer

Make a Beautiful Gift

[*Your Date and Time*]

Learn how to make beautiful painted glass globes
to use as ornaments or to give as gifts
All materials are provided for free.
Space is limited. Please register

At

[*Your Library*]
[*Your Address * Your Phone Number*]

Reasonable accommodation for individuals with disabilities is available.
Please contact the library prior to the event if you require accommodation.

For a turn-of-the-year program with no holiday associations, try an interpersonal relations seminar for teens. Approach a high school or middle school counselor, youth intervention coordinator, or the other staff of youth-serving agencies in your community and ask if they'd be willing to speak to teens at your library. Publicize the program through the school PTA and newsletter—most circulate one near the end of winter term and are willing to devote a few lines to a worthwhile library event. "Coping with Other People: Start the New Year with a Fresh Slate" is an appealing topic, because many teens both need and want to get along better with their parents, teachers, and peers.

role-playing game (whether fantasy, science fiction, or historical adventure) is a fun way to help teens hone group interaction skills and to provide camaraderie and imaginative play, but it does require serious storytelling skills on the part of the librarian moderating the game.

CONCLUSION

As you close your last program of the year, you're really getting ready to start all over again. You'll be gearing up with advertising and booktalk preparations to start that new Teen Book Discussion group and promote the new Printz Award. Many of the programs can be repeated (and will improve as you do so); people like rhythm. Repetition with variation feels natural to us.

More important, you've laid the groundwork for teen involvement in your library's programs. To some extent nothing makes (or breaks) library programming for teens so much as this. It can be hard to get started. I've worked in branches where this is a considerable challenge. Don't be discouraged. Getting your local teens involved and convincing them that the library has what they need and what they want (including library programs) is worth the time and effort.

Take some time, at the end of the each program you offer, to write up what worked and what didn't. Your checklist can include:

- *Publicity*: How did teens who attended hear about my program? Are my flyers reaching the intended audience? This is potentially the most useful piece of information as teens get their information either by word of mouth or by radio and TV. The latter two tend to be out of range of most library budgets.
- *Timing*: Am I scheduling programs that conflict with other things that teens either need or want to do? Get and keep handy a copy

of your local school's calendar. Many now have this information on the web. In whatever form it comes, check it before scheduling your programs.

- *Age-appropriate appeal*: Do my programs tie in to what teens are experiencing in their life? Teens might be getting a first job, a first car, or a first date. They're coping with relationships and trying to figure out who they are and what they want to do. Teens want real skills, and they want learning to be fun.

- *Can I afford to do this right?* More than once, my own enthusiasm and ambition (and that of my teen volunteers) have vaulted past real limitations of time and money.

- *It is time to retire the project?* Realize that even though each new group of teens faces the same challenges and joys that previous years' teens have faced, some programs are faddish in nature. They don't wear well. Others do, but *you* may burn out. If you've lost all interest in a program, you won't be able to sell it to teachers, parents, or teens.

As the year comes to an end, you know what worked and what didn't. You've gotten at least a few teens involved with the library, and you're psyched up to recruit many more. Now it's a whole new year.

BIBLIOGRAPHY

BOOKS AND TEXT

Professional Reading

Berg, Adriane G., and Arthur Berg Bochner. *The Totally Awesome Business Book for Kids: With 20 Super Businesses You Can Start Right Now*. New York: Newmarket Press, 1995.

Bodart, Joni Richards, ed. *Booktalk!*, vol. 5. New York: Wilson, 1993. Also: *Booktalk!*, vols. 1–4. See also her Booktalking listserv via *http://www.egroups.com*.

Brunvand, Jan Harold, Robert Loren Fleming, and Robert Boyd Jr. *The Big Book of Urban Legends*. New York: Paradox Press, 1994.

Carlson, Laura, Sean Creighton, and Sheila Cunningham, eds. *Literary Laurels: A Reader's Guide to Award-Winning Fiction*. New York: Hillyard, 1995.

Chase's Calendar of Events 2001: The Day-by-Day Directory to Special Days, Weeks and Months. Chicago: Contemporary Books, 2000.

Craughwell, Thomas J. *Alligators in Sewer: And 222 Other Urban Legends*. New York: Black Dog & Leventhal, distributed by Workman Publishing, 1999.

Gilson, Kristin, et al. *The Baby-Sitter's Nightmare: Tales Too Scary to Be True*. New York: HarperCollins, 1998.

Hersch, Patricia. *A Tribe Apart: A Journey into the Heart of American Adolescence*. New York: Fawcett Columbine, 1998.

Jones, Patrick. *Connecting Young Adults and Libraries*, 2nd ed. New York: Neal Schuman, 1998. See also The Connecting Young Adults and Libraries website: *http://www.connectingya.com/*.

Lingbloom, Evie Wilson. *Hanging Out at Rocky Creek: A Melodrama in Basic Young Adult Services in Public Libraries.* Metuchen, NJ: Scarecrow Press, 1994.

Littlejohn, Carol. *Talk That Book! Booktalks to Promote Reading.* Worthington, OH: Linworth Publishing, 1999.

Masters, Phil, Terry Pratchett, and Paul Kilby. *GURPS [Generic Universal Roleplaying System] Discworld.* Austin, TX: Steve Jackson Games, 1998.

Mooney, Julie, and the editors of Ripley's Entertainment. *The World of Ripley's Believe It or Not.* New York: Black Dog & Leventhal, 1999.

New York Public Library. *Books for the Teen Age.* New York: Office of the Branch Libraries, 1998.

Offner, Rose. *Journal to the Soul for Teenagers.* Berkeley, CA: Celestial Arts, 1999.

Schiffman, Stephan. *Cold Calling Techniques (That Really Work),* 4th ed. Holbrook, MA: Adams Media Corp., 1999. Skim past the moneymaking aspect of this book and focus on what it will teach you about making calls that get you meetings so that you can pitch your product—whether it's a booktalk or a program for teens.

VOYA: Voice of Youth Advocates Magazine. Lanham, MD: Scarecrow Press, 1978– .

Weiner, Steven. *100 Graphic Novels for Public Libraries.* Northampton, MA: Kitchen Sink Press, 1996.

Young Adult Fiction and Nonfiction

Bujold, Lois McMaster. *The Warrior's Apprentice.* New York: Baen Books, 1986.

Burnford, Sheila. *The Incredible Journey.* New York: Bantam Books, 1987.

Cheng, Lung and Jeff Yang. *I Am Jackie Chan: My Life in Action.* New York: Random House, 1998.

Cooney, Caroline. *The Face on the Milk Carton.* New York: Bantam, 1990.

Cooney, Caroline. *The Terrorist.* New York: Scholastic, 1997.

Crutcher, Chris. *Staying Fat for Sarah Byrnes.* New York: Greenwillow, 1993.

Duncan, Lois. *Don't Look Behind You.* New York: Delacorte, 1989.

Duncan, Lois. *Killing Mr. Griffin,* paperback ed. New York: Bantam Doubleday Dell, 1990.

Duncan, Lois. *Who Killed My Daughter?,* paperback ed. New York: Dell, 1994.

Farmer, Nancy. *The Ear, the Eye and the Arm.* New York: Puffin, 1995.

Hesse, Karen. *The Music of Dolphins,* paperback ed. New York: Apple, 1998.

Hobbs, Will. *Downriver.* New York: Atheneum, 1991.

Klause, Annette Curtis. *Blood and Chocolate.* New York: Bantam Books, 1997.

Klause, Annette Curtis. *The Silver Kiss.* New York: Delacorte, 1990.

Letts, Billie. *Where the Heart Is.* New York: Warner Books, 1995.

Levine, Gail Carson. *Ella Enchanted.* New York: HarperCollins Juvenile Books, 1997.

Lowry, Lois. *The Giver.* New York: Houghton Mifflin, 1993.

Mernissi, Fatima. *Dreams of Trespass: Tales of a Harem Girlhood,* paperback ed. Reading, MA: Addison-Wesley Longman, 1995.

Myers, Walter Dean. *Scorpions,* paperback ed. New York: HarperTrophy, 1990.

Paulsen, Gary. *The Schernoff Discoveries.* New York: Bantam Books, 1997.

Pennebaker, Ruth. *Don't Think Twice.* New York: Henry Holt, 1996.

Preston, Richard. *The Hot Zone*. New York: Anchor, 1995.

Talbot, Bryan. *The Tale of One Bad Rat*. Milwaukee, OR: Dark Horse Comics, 1995.

Thesman, Jean. *The Ornament Tree*, paperback ed. New York: Avon Books, 1998.

Thomas, Rob. *Rats Saw God*, paperback ed. New York: Aladdin Paperbacks, 1996.

Voigt, Cynthia. *Homecoming*. New York: Atheneum, 1981.

White, Rob. *Deathwatch*, paperback ed. New York: Laurel Leaf, 1993.

WEBSITES/ELECTRONIC

The Academy of American Poets sponsors National Poetry Month. Visit their website at *http://www.poets.org/npm/*.

The Alex Awards, which highlight the best adult books for young adults, can be found at *http://www.ala.org/yalsa/booklists/alex/*. The Alex Awards are sponsored by the Young Adult Library Services Association (YALSA) of the American Library Association (ALA).

The American Red Cross website is at *http://www.redcross.org*. Look for the links to "Courses for Children" (these include teens) and "Community Programs" as well as links to contact information for your local chapter of the Red Cross.

The Archie McFee & Company website, *http://www.archiemcphee.com/*, sells strange, goofy, and often inexpensive novelty items that are great for teen prizes.

The Association of American Publishers Website can be found at *http://www.publishers.org/home/index.htm*. Look for a link to its "Get Caught Reading" promotional toolkit.

Behind the Name website, *http://behindthename.com/*, provides the etymology and history of first names.

Booktalking listserv moderated by Joni Richards Bodart at *http://www.egroups.com* may be joined by registering with Egroups and searching for "booktalking."

Button machine sources on-line include Badge-A-Minit, at *http://www.badge-a-minit.com/*, and Dr. Don's Buttons, *http://www.buttonsonline.com*.

The Connecting Young Adults and Libraries website, by Patrick Jones, is located at *http://www.connectingya.com/*.

CPN: The College Planning Network at *http://www.collegeplan.org/* serves the Pacific Northwest.

CSS [College Scholarship Services]/Financial Aid Profile is available from the College Board at *http://www.collegeboard.org/finaid/fastaff/profile/html/indx000.html*.

Diamond Comics website is at *http://www.diamondcomics.com*. Diamond is the largest comic book distributor in the United States and is quite willing to set up library accounts.

The DoubleDog Press website at *http://www.dbldog.com/default.htm* sells Mystery Kits for children and young adults.

The Evil Overlord list created by Peter Anspach at *http://home.kscable.com/tung/overlord1.htm* contains parodies and lists of "what not to do."

FAFSA: Free Application for Federal Student Aid from the U.S. Department of Education forms may be found at *http://www.ed.gov/offices/OPE/express.html*.

Greyhound Friends Northwest at *www.halcyon.com/greyhnds/* is a local greyhound rescue group for western Washington State. For national links to your local greyhound rescue group, visit *http://www.adopt-a-greyhound.org*, website of the Greyhound Project Incorporated.

The Henna Page at *http://www.hennapage.com* is a source of information about henna body decorations. The site has an extensive collection of links to henna sites, including those selling commercial kits for do-it-yourself types.

Humane Society of the United States, *http://www.hsus.org/*, has links to regional offices and to local agencies.

The IRS website includes publications on-line as well as links to state income tax forms on-line. The site at *http://www.irs.gov/forms_pubs/pubs/index.htm* contains Publication 4, "Student's Guide to Federal Income Tax."

The Jersey Zoo, a part of the Jersey Wildlife Protection Trust, can be found online at *http://www.durrell.org/zoo/*.

Lois Duncan's author website is located at *http://www.iag.net/~barq/lois.html*.

The Michael L. Printz Award, *http://www.ala.org/yalsa/printz/*, is awarded annually for excellence in Young Adult literature and is sponsored by YALSA.

The Mystery Writers of America, Inc., website at *http://www.mysterywriters.net/* has links to Edgar Award winners, including the Edgar for best Young Adult mystery.

The National Association for Humane and Environmental Education website is *http://www.nahee.org*.

The National Storytelling Association may be contacted by mail (see chapter 10) or via its associated website: The National Storytelling Membership Association at *http://www.storynet.org/nsa/aboutnsa.htm*.

NetNoir is one of the leading black portals to the web. Its February "Black History Month" information and links are splendid: *http://www.netnoir.com*.

Pubyac is a listserv for all public librarians serving youth, including children and young adults. To subscribe, send an e-mail message to *list-proc@prairienet.org*. Leave the subject line blank. For the message, type: subscribe pubyac. The Pubyac homepage may be found at *http://www.pallasinc.com/pubyac*.

Say Hello to the World via the Internet Public Library at *http://www.ipl.org/youth/hello/*. Greetings in dozens of world languages (including some nonverbal ones) are presented in written and audio format.

The Seattle Thunderbirds website is at *http://www.mcneel.com/users/Tbirds/*.

Stumpers-List, the ultimate listserv for reference librarians around the world, has a website at *http://www.cuis.edu/~stumpers/*.

"Tattooing & Body Piercing: Decision Making for Teens" on the Virtual Hospital website, *http://www.vh.org/Patients/IHB/Derm/Tattoo/*, is a service of University of Iowa Healthcare.

Teen Advisory Board websites may be found for the Appleton (Wisconsin) Public Library at *http://teen.apl.org/TAB/*, the Arlington County (Virginia) Department of Libraries at *http://www.co.arlington.va.us/lib/teen/tab.htm*, the Pasco County (Florida) Library System at *http://power.pasco.lib.fl.us/teen_*

volunteer.html, and the Bay County (Michigan) Library at *http://www. baycountylibrary.org/TeenPage/teenboard.htm*.

The Teen Read Week website at *http://www.ala.org/teenread/* is sponsored by YALSA.

Urban Legend Reference Pages are at *http://www.snopes.com/ulindex.htm*. They provide the definitive source for information about urban legends and strange-but-true stories.

U.S. Chess On-line at *http://www.uschess.org/* is maintained by the U.S. Chess Federation. U.S. Chess On-line also provides links to local chess clubs.

The Washington Commission for the Humanities website may be found at *http:// www.humanities.org/*.

Wizard Magazine On-Line is at *http://store.yahoo.com/wizardworld/*. The magazine is devoted to comics, trading cards, and associated media.

Wizards of the Coast Online, *http://www.wizards.com/*, can help you link to local retail stores and to tournament information.

The X-Files official website is located at *http://www.thex-files.com/*.

YALSA's *Best Books for Young Adults* and other great booklists may be found at *http://www.ala.org/yalsa/booklists*.

Yalsa-bk is an open list for book discussion and other issues with teenage reading and Young Adult literature. To subscribe to yalsa-bk, send an e-mail message to *listproc@ala.org*. Leave the subject line blank. For the message, type: subscribe yalsa-bk Your-first-name Your-last-name. For more YALSA listservs, visit *http://www.ala.org/yalsa/professional/yalsalists.html*.

The Youth Art Month website is sponsored by the Council for Art Education. Contact *http://www.acminet.org/youth_art_month.htm* to get the name and contact points for your state's Youth Art Month chairperson, for local assistance, and for a free booklet of programming ideas.

INDEX

About the Author

KIRSTEN EDWARDS is a Young Adult Librarian for the King County
Library System in Duvall, Washington, and a member of the Washington
Library Association. This is her first book.